I0118595

On *Peace and War and Peace*

The selections in this collection are reminiscent of the free verse of old, often-quite-indecorous, rambling blues. In their totality they offer us text that is somehow simultaneously prosaic and poetic, strikingly powerful and sweetly tender, gently nuanced and stunningly blunt, inspiring and challenging as it explores the dark side of consciousness (in Jungian terms, the darkworld and the Shadow) and the light side, as well.

To adapt Charles Baudelaire's description of a new form of writing he termed a poetic prose: these texts, musical although lacking regular rhythms or definable rhyme schemes, are supple and jostling enough to accommodate themselves to the soul's lyrical movements, to musing's fluctuations, to sudden leaps of consciousness.

Peace and War and Peace offers a tribute to peace and a careful vision of war, rage, and violence. Fresh, inspiring, superb!

Joseph L. Kieff, Literary Critic.

Peace and War and Peace is a masterful collection of meditative poems on violence and war and love. Each of its poems offers the opportunity for one's consciousness to be deeply transformed. This compelling volume, while constituting a most sober reflection on war, reflective of a lifetime of experience and study, is an illumination upon the sanctity of life. A most fitting example is the poem, *Anger*, and its dedication to the Venerable Thich Quang Duc, the great spiritual warrior of the Vietnamese People.

David Slier, Ph.D., Fellow, American Academy of Traumatic Stress, provides combat-related treatments at the Naval Medical Center San Diego. Dr. Slier, a Marine Combat Veteran – Vietnam '67, coordinated and participated in the memorial service at the Naval Medical Center San Diego, 2 July 2010, commemorating Vietnam-War-related events on 2 July 1967, the single worst day of causalities for the Marine Corps in the Vietnam War.

"Why war?" asked Freud. "Why not peace?" enquires Ginsberg. Investigating this issue, he brings along his immense knowledge of Eastern and Western philosophies, although leaving them deliberately in a chiaroscuro background. Instead of proposing a treatise, he writes in evocative verses and aphorisms. This freedom of poetry goes hand in hand with the rigor he brings to his object.

Ginsberg consistently presents his work and himself as a reality-in-process—not unlike Mondrian (assiduously reworking his impeccable abstractions) or Montaigne (infinitely reworking his precise self-observations).

Ginsberg peeks through the forest as he also focuses upon the trees (and even the twigs): our emotional ups and downs, clarities and confusion, symptom-formation, the unconscious, aggressivity and self-aggression, our lethal compulsion to repeat painful patterns, so resistant to change, and the work of psychotherapy to handle such a lifelong task. With his own acute sense of civilization (and its discontents), Ginsberg looks upon societal development (or lack thereof), in the light of our staccato development of self-awareness and self-understanding. He nods to the multiple selves (that point to our elusive self), to the I/you dyad (to "others" and to our ever-so problematic attachments). In so doing, he portrays in suggestive strokes the flux of our moods, as they interweave with the language, the culture, and the society in which they arise. He underscores the feelings and the emotions of our dark side, in shame and guilt and guilt and shame, rage and anger and anger and rage, along with the defense mechanisms inherent in them. Without denying these, he looks for the synergy of our dark side with our "better angels," whenever we feel and act, moved by humility, peacefulness, compassion or love.

To limit this comment to Western history, we may suggest in broad strokes that some philosophers (Kant, Hegel, et al.) wish to construct systems of thought. Others (Nietzsche, Derrida, et al.) shun the systemic and the universal to make the case for the particular. Ginsberg seems closer to Pascal's style: His poetic presentation shares with Pascal the conceptual art of the "fragment," the fragment as it aims, in pointillistic manner, to convoke the reader to co-construct an ineffable coherent whole. Thus, reading the free poetry of *Peace and War and Peace* is therapeutic inasmuch as it invites the reader to participate in an art of life and to enjoy the "music of the spheres."

Alain J.-J. Cohen,
Professor of Comparative Literature and Film Studies
at UCSD (University of California, San Diego) and
member of SDPSI (San Diego Psychoanalytic Society and Institute).

Ginsberg's poetic voice in *Peace and War and Peace* is quite wonderful. There is a very calm and vibrant rhythm to the movement of both sound and meaning. And there are hints—no, a membrane, the vibration of the instrument—that resonate with the voice of Sufi poets, in being both profoundly intimate and, at the same time, universal and impersonal.

I love this cover and the appeal to compassion for those caught up in war and the deep injuries suffered. It frames these poems beautifully.

Yvonne Simon.

Ginsberg has the ability to describe the world from numerous perspectives. Although each perspective appears to have a specific source, the sentiments in each poem are so profoundly universal that even the most personal of confessions proclaims a truth of humanity. He portrays his emotions as well as his observations based in historical fact, psychology, and political science, as well as the experiences of human life. Some of his poems step through language barriers. Ginsberg uses words and phrases from different cultures and languages (which he subsequently translates into English for the reader) to further examine his own thoughts.

The primary accomplishment of *Peace and War and Peace* is the gentle, but unavoidable self-reflection that the reader experiences. By highlighting known (and subtle) truths of society, the world, and human nature, his poems insist that the reader turn inward toward his or her own personal truths, as well as seeing the world through Ginsberg's eyes. At once self-reflective, informative, and activist, his poems create an experience for the reader that forces one to think about human nature and the importance of peace. Ginsberg seldom criticizes specific events directly, but rather explains the universal problems of war, the damage that society both inflicts and ignores, as well as the beauty and tragedy that comes from human life. Although the book does not proclaim to be overtly existential, his work supplements the work of existential, humanistic, and transpersonal studies and their perspectives of human nature. All of these points of view are evident in these reports on a lifetime of observation, experience, and emotional helping.

Each poem carefully explores a specific aspect of experience, be it a battlefield in war, a personal feeling of loss, a moment from a love relationship, or an observation of an individual's responsibility to society. In a time when information is frequently contradictory and analysis often muddled, Ginsberg's poetry encourages his readers to slow down, reflect, and open their minds to the inner and outer world.

The poems are well-written, well-conceived, and easy to understand. Ginsberg displays a singular ability to describe complex concepts and experiences in few words with the aim of creating vivid and deep understanding for the reader. Social activists, writers, psychotherapists, and those participating in psychotherapy can glean a great deal of insight and inspiration from this poetic collection.

Carrie V. Pate, Saybrook University.

Remarks for the Reader

These vignettes or verbal illuminations (cousins, perhaps, to the medieval literary art form of illuminated manuscripts) are sketches of a variety of landscapes of the mind, a cartography of the heart in transformation, evoking specific life situations and related mind states and mental processes.

Making use of a concentrated structure that has been called free poetry, poetic prose, prosaic poetry, and evocative verse, these vignette-poems consist of miniature illuminations of consciousness in forms reflecting peace and war, mundane joy and rage.

Following these, in the closing parts of the book, a fresh vision is presented (alluded to by the final "peace" of the title) that evokes another consciousness, one that is more calm, clear, and loving (to borrow the title of a companion book of mine).

Searching into the experienced roots of our tendencies to agitation, anxiety, fear, confusion, and violence, encouraging a compassionate appreciation of the difficulties that people experience, both in times of peace and especially in times of war, this collection seeks to illustrate these realities, inviting the promising shift to a more harmonious world.

This passionate search for more comprehensive and elegant alternatives to our usual ways of thinking and acting in the seemingly endless alternating of peace and war is an ultimately vital, crucial endeavor aimed at distilling inspired, grounding wisdom from the initially inarticulate depths of our raw experience.

Mitchell D. Ginsberg
January 2015

Peace and War and Peace

Also by Mitchell D. Ginsberg

Mind and Belief:
Psychological Ascription and the Concept of Belief

The Far Shore:
Vipassanā, The Practice of Insight

The Inner Palace:
Mirrors of Psychospirituality
in Divine and Sacred Wisdom-Traditions

Calm, Clear, and Loving:
Soothing the Distressed Mind,
Healing the Wounded Heart

Mindful Raft over Troubled Waters

Peace and War and Peace
The Heart in Transformation

Second Edition

Mitchell D. Ginsberg

Wisdom Moon Publishing
2015

PEACE AND WAR AND PEACE
THE HEART IN TRANSFORMATION

Second Edition, 2015

© 2012 Mitchell D. Ginsberg
New material, © 2015 Mitchell D. Ginsberg

All rights reserved. Tous droits réservés.

No part of this work may be copied, reproduced, recorded, stored, or translated, in any form, or transmitted by any means electronic, mechanical, or other, whether by photocopy, fax, email, internet group postings, or otherwise, without written permission from the copyright holder, *except for brief quotations* in reviews for a magazine, journal, newspaper, broadcast, podcast, etc., or in scholarly or academic papers, *when quoted with a full citation to this work.*

Published by Wisdom Moon Publishing LLC
San Diego, CA, USA

Wisdom Moon™, the Wisdom Moon logo™, *Wisdom Moon Publishing*™, and *WMP*™ are trademarks of Wisdom Moon Publishing LLC.

www.WisdomMoonPublishing.com

ISBN 978-1-938459-54-2 (softcover, alk. paper)
ISBN 978-1-938459-56-6 (eBook)

LCCN 2015931447

Front cover photo: digitally adapted from a photograph taken during the Weimar Republic, in Berlin, 1923, stored at the Deutsches Bundesarchiv (German Federal Archive), Accession Number: Bild 146-1972-062-01.

Peace and War and Peace
The Heart in Transformation

I. Peace and War and Peace

❧   ❧   ❧   ❧

II. Life and Death and Life

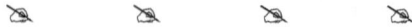

     🕊   🕊   🕊   🕊

III. Through the Faces of Rage

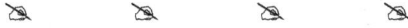

    🖎   🖎   🖎   🖎

IV. Faces of War

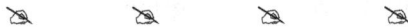

    🖎   🖎   🖎   🖎

V. There is a Goodness

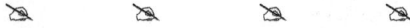

☙   ☙   ☙   ☙

VI. Restlessness Ceases

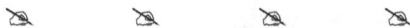

☙   ☙   ☙   ☙

VII. Understanding Within and Without

❧   ❧   ❧   ❧

❧   ❧   ❧   ❧

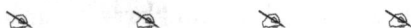

❧   ❧   ❧   ❧

Dedication Page

To all those in my life who have shown me their love and treated me with respect, my appreciative indebtedness.

To all those in my life who have allowed me to show them my love and to treat them with respect, my gratitude.

With a special dedication to
Milton M. Dobkin (January 16, 1922-July 13, 1944).
Second Lieutenant, Navigator, USAAF, US Army Air Forces,
Eighth Air Force, 2nd Bombardment Division,
96th Combat Bombardment Wing (Heavy),
466th Bombardment Group (Heavy),
787th Bombardment Squadron (6L).
Killed when the Consolidated B-24 Liberator bomber he was navigating took off from RAF Attlebridge Airfield (USAAF name: Station #120) and then crashed near Rackheath, just north of Norwich, Norfolk, UK, a brief flight of perhaps 5 miles—the plane's wings unable to support the fuel and bomb loads, given its perilously too-heavily-armored fuselage ... and this, well after the late 1942 confrontation when Glenn L. Martin indicated no intention to correct the frequently-fatal inadequate wing-support design of his Martin B-26 Marauder (nicknamed the Widow-maker, the Flying Cigar, the Flying Coffin, Martin's Murderer, the B-Dash-Crash, the Murdering Marauder, and, punning, with gallows humor, the Martin Miss Carriage), until Senator Harry Truman replied that in that case the Senate Committee of which he was Chairman would see to it that no defective B-26s would be purchased; PS: as reported in Truman's *Memoirs*, Martin agreed on the spot to make aeronautical changes (the B-26-10 began production in January 1943, with changes to engine and propellers, wingspread increased to 71 feet, the vertical stabilizer/tail-wing fin now 21.5 feet, & so on). Sadly, a lesson lost, not taken as a precedent for the B-24's similar lethal problems.

I remember Uncle Milton throwing me, a joyful baby, up toward the ceiling in the large home where all 11 of us in our 3-generation family lived together; at the time of his death (I was 2 by then), he was 22.

He was one of many, in one of many wars.

Peace and War and Peace

Nestor: My friends, warriors, ... now ... let us slay the men; afterwards, at leisure you shall plunder the armor from the corpses that lie dead over the plain.

Homer, *The Iliad* (8th or 7th Century BCE), Book 6.66-71.

For no one is so foolish as to choose war rather than peace, since in peace sons bury their fathers, but in war, fathers bury their sons.

Herodotus (484?-425? BCE), *The Histories* (440 BCE), Book 1.87.

It is sweet and becoming to die for one's country.

Horace (65-8 BCE), *Odes* (23 BCE), III.2.13.

Here is a case of law to examine: It is prohibited to kill; every killer is punished, unless he has killed in great military campaigns, and to the sound of trumpets: this is the rule.

François-Marie Arouet, known as Voltaire (1694-1778),
Dictionnaire philosophique (1764), from entry for DROIT.
Droit des gens, droit naturel. SECTION PREMIÈRE.

My first wish is, to see this plague to Mankind [War] banished from the Earth; & the Sons and daughters of this World employed in more pleasing & innocent amusements than in preparing implements, & exercising them for the destruction of the human race.

George Washington (1732-1799), letter to David Humphreys,
written at Mount Vernon, July 25, 1785. Original orthography.

To delight in war is a merit in the soldier, a dangerous quality in the captain, and a positive crime in the statesman.... Nevertheless, ... the glories of war are all blood-stained, delirious, and infected with crime; the combative instinct is a savage prompting by which one man's good is found in another's evil.

George Santayana, né
Jorge Augustín Nicolás Ruiz de Santayana y Borrás (1863-1952),
Reason in Society (1905), pp. 84-85.

The great crime in war is that man kills man, made in the image of God, ... war is not simply a wrong, ... it is the great crime of civilization, the killing of men by men like wild beasts.

Andrew Carnegie (1835-1919), from his address *The Moral Issue Involved in War*, given at the Conference of the American Society for Judicial Settlement of International Disputes, held at the New Willard Hotel, Washington D.C., on December 15, 1910.

Who cared for the men who had risked their lives and bore on their bodies the scars of war? The pensions doled out to blinded soldiers would not keep them alive. The consumptives, the gassed, the paralyzed, were forgotten in institutions where they lay hidden from the public eye.

Sir Philip Gibbs (1877-1962), *Realities of War* (1920), p. 448.

Let's not talk high-sounding phrases. Let's not use old words, shop-worn words, words like "glory" and "peace," without thinking just exactly what they mean. There's no "glory" in killing. There's no "glory" in maiming men.

General John J. Pershing (1860-1948), Commander-in-Chief of the AEF, the American Expeditionary Forces in Europe (1917-1919), quoted in *The New York Times*, Sept. 7, 1924, p. XX3.

Why, of course, the *people* don't want war. Why would some poor slob on a farm want to risk his life in a war when the best that he can get out of it is to come back to his farm in one piece. Naturally, the common people don't want war; neither in Russia nor in England nor in America, nor for that matter in Germany. That is understood. But, after all, it is the *leaders* of the country who determine the policy and it is always a simple matter to drag the people along, whether it is a democracy or a fascist dictatorship or a Parliament or a Communist dictatorship....

[Oh, but] the people can always be brought to the bidding of the leaders. That is easy. All you have to do is tell them they are being attacked and denounce the pacifists for lack of patriotism and exposing the country to danger. It works the same way in any country.

Reichsmarschall Hermann Goering (1893-1946), in private conversation with Gustave M. Gilbert (U.S. Military Chief Psychologist at the Nuremberg Trials) on April 18, 1946, as reported in Gilbert's *Nuremberg Diary* (1947), pp. 278-279.

☉ ☉

... love is somehow [even in Auschwitz] the ultimate and the highest to which human existence can soar.

Viktor E. Frankl (1905-1997), *Ein Psycholog erlebt das Konzentrationslager* (1946), p. 53.

Nothing is so whole as a shattered heart.

Attributed to Nachman of Breslav (Ukraine, 1772-1810) and to Menachem Mendel of Kotzk (Poland, 1787-1859).

... friendship ... is, moreover, an absolute essential for a happy life, since without friends no man would choose to live, even if he possessed every other good thing.

Aristotle (384-322 BCE),
Nicomachean Ethics **(350 BCE), Book 8, Chap. 1, 1155a3-6.**

Follow your wise heart [*ib*] for as long as you live.

**Attributed to Ptaḥ-Ḥotep (ancient Pharaonic Egypt,
Fifth Dynasty of the Old Kingdom, circa 2400 BCE),
in a rendering of the hieroglyphic text of his maxims
(the Prisse papyrus, Line 186, being Column 7, Line 9,
elsewhere cited as Maxim 11, Line 1).**

I. Peace and War and Peace

Peace and war and peace

Will we one day truly taste the bitterness of learning war
and being fed up with it finally plow it under?
Or will we impatiently fill every void in our wisdom
with the old reliable sword of wrathful violence?
Shall it be oh noble friends peace or shall it be war?
Shall this world be a sharp-barbed vale of tears
or the Place of radiant awe and sacred mutual caring?

Stopping smartly here to look ahead now
in centuries to come
we will be quite gone fully forgotten
        will be but ashes but dust.

Others fresh in spirit luscious in flesh will love;
will flowers not blossom?
Will the sun not set
despite our follies
the moon not rise
will nightingales not sing forth?

Hatreds though will flare once again
wars may well be fought with new
dead
wounded
survivors
weary widows wandering children lost widowers
mournful childless (child-lost soul-ripped) parents
war's inverse orphans in an unnatural inferno.

Still others
some in innocent ignorant bliss
some somewhat sensing but not appreciating
some fully remembering yet ready to start again
in this heaven-hell (the bravest of us all)
will celebrate the roses and thorns of a natural bouquet,
will find love and joy,
despite and because of it all.

Yearning for transformation: psychospirituality

Psychospirituality:
the profound evolution of consciousness,
its radical transformation,
in accordance with inspired ideals.

Its questions ～

What is actually happening to me here?

What is troubling me, disturbing me?

How can I develop greater clarity,
insightful understanding, grounded security,
loving kindness, gentle wisdom?

How can I be more at peace,
inspired, creative, fulfilled?

In this turmoil, what can I
with tenderness appreciate
about the longings
and values of my heart?

What do I see of my own humanity, my honesty,
my desire for my best self,
my most honorable, noble, and wise self?

How can I develop my greatest potential?

Beyond my childhood, beyond my family,
beyond my experiences, adventures, boredoms, and crises,
beyond even my land, my society, my culture,
what are my deepest and highest qualities?

And in this same light,
what can I see of others' similar highest nature?

Here in society,
what can we appreciate of our interactions,

4

the ways we touch impact influence nourish challenge
one another, opening up new visions
of who we are, what it is to be alive?

And in this same light,
what can we see of our connection and interaction
with the entire universe surrounding us
the sacred Nature in which we live
the divine Place in which everything occurs?

Or, staying with our body,
can we slow down to feel awe at the breeze
moving leaves and branches and on our skin
to behold sublime beauty before our eyes
to savor quiet tears running down our face
to sense the subtle magnificence of tenderness?

And in seeing that it's perfect, may we not go blind:
do we see what is truly perfect *and* truly imperfect
about the perfection, embrace its wholeness *and* its cracks?

Then, even if as is said there is nothing to achieve,
may this core yearning of psychospirituality be realized:

May we each and all experience a personal transformation
to a soulful, integrated completeness of heart-and-mind.

May I, may we all,
experience and nurture
this great potential we each and all have,
in this very lifetime.

Psychospiritual companionship

Conversation is for this purpose,
consultation is for this purpose,
getting close is for this purpose,
listening is for this purpose ～
for the clinging-free liberation of consciousness.

This may be compared with the perspective expressed in the ancient passage found in the Pāli Canon (the *Tipiṭaka* or *Three Baskets*), in the *Vinaya-Piṭaka* or *Basket of Sangha Regulations*, in its vol. 5, at p. 164 (Vin.v.164). That passage, in Pāli, is quoted and discussed at pp. 175-176 in M. Ginsberg, *Calm, Clear, and Loving.*

"... the fulfillment of consciousness with idealistic conceptions is characteristic for Western theosophy, but not the confrontation with the shadow and the darkworld. One does not, however, become more light by imagining the light but rather by making the dark more conscious. The latter, though, is unpleasant and therefore not popular."

Carl Gustav Jung (1875-1961), *Der philosophische Baum* (1945), revised edition in *Von den Wurzeln des Bewußtseins: Studien über den Archetypus* (1954), pp. 351-496, translated from text at pp. 369-370.

Transformation: through darkness to light

Through the years
I see you shift

from fear and doubt and confusion
wondering what it's all about,
whether it's worth it at all,
with bouts of frustration and rage and fatigue
beyond your years,

to calm and confidence
coming
gradually
surely

though
      NOT at all   STRAIGHT
            (we know)   A
                    IN   LINE

to realize your deepest desires
to live your dreams
of fulfillment, of inner harmony, of achievement,
of love and intimate human contact,
of security and adventure,
of sweet and even joyous moments that make it
beautifully clear deliciously clear
that life is indeed worth living.

May this journey be the fortune of the world.

7

On appreciating transformations of the heart

Describing the heart in transformation ～
the roots and the branches of its bare movements ～
presents for you portrayals of the heart
alternatingly compassionate critical muted mirthful
wrathful raw rough refined yearning or calm.

Writers
(even a cartographer of the heart)
speak through our texts or our fictional characters
luring you into our worlds visions creations
at times our language and its richness tone voice
rhythms rhymes alliterations
enticing your minds hearts even souls.

A poem's poignant perspective
personalities in a play or novel
value-laden political papers
(even these maps portrayals word sketches
of the heart's peregrinations):
all experiments in the imagination
inviting you to experience
from the viewpoint of the mindset laid out for you.

Literary offerings here at hand or afar
poetically evocative
present you with experiences in the imagination.

II. Life and Death and Life

We are creatures

We are creatures of clarity and confusion
of soaring imagination and sleepy boredom
of fresh perception and stale prejudice
of passion and peace
of love and hate and indifference
of longing and of fulfillment.

We are difficult and we are easy.
We rush ahead
driven to some unseen unknown end and
we take our calming time to savor each instant.

We are beings of fear and of courage
of pride and shame
of adventure and security
of reassuring habit and exciting spontaneity
of doubt and of certainty.

We want it all and we can let it all go.
We are this and much more.
We are this and much less.
We are creatures of life and of death.
We are here and we are gone.
We are complex and we are simple.

Life and death and life

Somewhere someone is dying
after a long full life,
a slow process, an all-too-fast process.

The end is close, everyone can sense.

Family coming from
very nearby from
quite far away.

Hoping to have
a last moment
to express love,
appreciation,
thankfulness,
forgiveness,
to ask for forgiveness,
to reassure,
to come to resolution,
to laugh together,
to cry together.

Then,
a gentle death
in the caring arms of the belovèd.
Quiet moments, last words,
loving tenderness,
full consciousness, absence of pain.
What more could be hoped for?

After the death
the last rites.
Some are sobbing,
some are moaning.
Tears and mucus flow.

Some look stressed, stiff, stonefaced,
stuffed, packed, painfully constipated,
alas,

and some relieved,
some simply exhausted.

Family members gather
close to one another,
marking sub-clan splits.
Some won't even talk with,
won't look at
certain others.

Some sob in the arms of others,
some stand stoically alone or in group formation.

Food and drink are offered.
Some drink to feel relief.
Others have no urge to drink,
not even thirst.

Some have lost all appetite
while others are eating
as if food will revive the departed.
Some are
emerging from a time of no appetite
during those last trying days.

Some contemplate property and wealth,
hoping for some share of an inheritance.

Some review the years of shared times now
gone forever symbolically soon
to be buried deep in the ground
or cremated up in smoke.

The children of those present
play in the background nearby,
innocently, naively, freely, gayly.

What a joy

Clear awareness creates a deep poetry,
leads us to heartfelt appreciation of life
to a sense of deep peace
to connectedness with the universe.

Here, we may investigate together
some varieties of human experience
to appreciate the role experience plays in life
(a phenomenon of finite length),
to savor consciousness and awareness,
the contact between us and others,
the joy simply to be alive ∽
all rare quite temporary gifts.

The unpredictable course of life unfolds through time,
a unique reality, a mosaic evolving moment by moment,
inviting our ongoing appreciation,
to see each turn in our road,
to appreciate each step we now take (the present),
its greater meaning for us depending on where
we have been (the past) and where
we will next find ourselves (the future).

How vibrantly intense when we take care to live fully,
to be open to all of our experience ∽ not only what fits
into our ideas of the world (our "being realistic"), or
into our ideas of a proper, correct, or enlightened life
(our "being good").
Open and clear in our perception,
fully experiencing and respecting
each moment and situation in our overall journey
makes possible our feeling creative, alert, light, flexible,
open to life's intense and rich possibilities.

I can't let go

I can't let go.
I don't want to let go.
I want to keep this moment.
It is too important
to me for me to
let it disappear and
be forgotten.
What do I want here?
A joy I want to re-experience.
A moment to savor.
A problem to resolve.
An issue to clarify.
A relationship to preserve,
conserve, contain,
maintain,
resolve, dissolve.
But the world has its own
plans and tempo and changes
(ah, uninvited impermanence)
that are not in synch
with my interests
preferences
personal needs.
Harmonizing
the personal
and its life context the extra-personal
the inner
and the outer
a creative quest, not a given.

In this world

In this world
with its harshness
and violence
its carelessness
and its couldntcarelessness

we

who can do what we can do
but cannot do what we cannot do ～

it's time to admit our limits to make the world perfect
to repair the cracks in the world, as one tradition puts it.

It is said we must try even if we see it as impossible

perhaps after all we are wrong (about what is impossible)
perhaps what we do

even if not complete
makes things better

a lightening of the heavy bitterness of life
of someone's soul perhaps

or else we could cry more tears
than the waters of all of the world's oceans.
Which, as the Buddha pointed out,
we have done already
and will perhaps do again.

"… in the end one must begin to love in order not to become ill, and one must fall ill if as a result of rejection one is unable to love."

Sigmund Freud (1856-1939), "Zur Einführung des Narzißmus," *Jahrbuch der Psychoanalyse*, vol. 6 (1914), pp. 1-24, translated from text at p. 11.

We learn to close off

We learn to close off
be neat tight carefully circumspect
inner warmth hidden
caring hidden
concern hidden
hesitation hidden
fear hidden
yearning hidden
love hidden
as if that's a favor to someone
as if we need to save these for later.

Everyone's loss.

This is the dharma

This is the dharma:
the way the world works.
This is the Buddha-dharma:
the way the world works
according to the Buddha's
insights.
We are born and in our
body and in our
mind ～
a series of pains, illnesses,
worries, hopes, dreams,
frustrations.
Of friendships, joys, betrayals,
projects created, of
projects fulfilled or not.
Of aging, if not dying young.
And somewhere
most definitely
death.
And yet
in this world of sorrows,
warmth and tenderness and peace are
waiting for us
if we see through all
the rest of this world to them.

We are rich within ourselves

We are rich within ourselves ~
when we contact all of our own visions and perspectives
we are already in a crowd of realities
a motley crowd
a crowd of opinions hopes fears satisfactions dreams
features to recognize to harmonize to integrate.

With this
we can search elsewhere
without closing off from our
own interconnected completeness
finding then with another
a doubly rich fullness.

Torn from my land

1   Torn from my land,
roots longing for their ground,
images pull at my heart,
tingle my eyes,
and ∿ short of breath ∿
one deep gasping sigh.

Friends reach out.
The warmth nourishes
my confused
bowels.

2   You are gone.
My future
has disappeared.
How has Destiny
robbed me
of my comfort and
of my ∿ (oh, this loss words cannot capture or contain)?

3   How can you (I)
go on
oblivious
to all the pain
your (my) numb activity
has engendered?

4   Years have
en passant
opened and
closed possibilities
of life.
You were here
and in my memory and heart
you are here still.
What means more
from our life's viewpoint
than camaraderie?
You enrich my life,

in your presence, in your absence.
Can I thank you enough?

5   I can see but a little
of what you
have given me.
I am not blind.
My vision
is simply finite.

6   To lose one's twin
one's soul-
mate
and
live neither
forgetting nor stagnating:
this not easy.

7   Can you be newborn
alive to the life you now live
and yet
let the past
have its place,
neither resisted nor a wallowing place?

8   If I were a flea in your ear
I could hear every thought
and every question,
every query
and every answer.
Lucky flea
unlucky me.

We can watch our worthlessness

We can watch our worthlessness.

Here is where we believe our thoughts
declaring our worthlessness,
official dispatches from our
Ministry of Propaganda's
Bureau of Self-Deprecation.

Not staying here, but reaching out
for expansiveness of mind,
we can watch our thoughts
declaring our worthlessness,
and watch them disappear
and end.

We can watch our thoughts
declaring our worthlessness
disappear and end,
and see our breathing
which survives beyond
these thoughts.

We can see our breathing
that survives beyond
these thoughts,
and see that we too
are beyond these thoughts
and beyond this breathing.

This place is expansive and
calm,
peaceful and
gentle.

Wisdom is not cocky

Wisdom is not cocky
nor snide.
It is free of condescension
and insult.
Its expression can be inspiring
and expansive.
Wisdom does not seek
self-aggrandizement
at the expense of the audience.
It is offered
as a gift, free of disdain.
It is not a burden to accept.
Wisdom takes insight
and marries it with compassion,
with respectful good-will.
Wisdom sees the forest and the trees.
It is a gift
for all who receive it
to savor and celebrate and
for those who offer it freely
with an open hand, as was said of the Buddha.

The day has drawn to a close

The day has drawn to a close.
Night is upon us.
We get through each day in
ways we see only at the end.

And if we look back
we can
draw opinions about the day
now gone but can also stay
in the quiet presence of
the heartbeat
ready for bed
ready for sleep
ready for another day.

At the entrance

The doorway is open, but I dare not enter.
I remain where I am,
feeling the exquisite possibilities.

Pausing ∼
as when we stop our tasks in the late afternoon,
hear the soft refreshing breeze
passing by the leaves of trees,
see the branches bending gently,
feel it on our body,
cooling and relaxing,
its subtlety quieting us into vibrant calm.

Not rushing in
not rushing through,
I feel the nectar
and vibrate to sensual energies held in check.

Delicious restraint.

Softly she signals then
her open welcoming.

Cast your net wide

Cast your net wide, my dear seekers.
Seek love not knowing where
it will show itself, whether
in bright meadows
moments of glee
dreary chambers
moments of stress.
Then bring it forth
into your deepest heart
to let it take root and flourish
down in your very depths.

Fly, my dears

Fly, my dears;
breathe the pure air of the heights;
see the world anew;
float in the joy of freedom.

Stay grounded,
feet on the soft supporting earth,
to appreciate
every single breath
every heartbeat
every experience
every moment of this precious life of yours.

When you keep in touch
even from afar
we will take joy in each moment of your happiness
and have sympathy for
each moment of faltering
you may encounter
on your uncharted paths.

These are your paths to discover
after all
not another's to define for you.

This is the way
of love free of demands.

How I long for your truth

How I long for your truth,
the palpable presence of your innermost being,

this entrance
into your mind and heart and soul
that touches me with its undeniable reality,
responding to my own meager attempts,
my own signs and signals and manifestos mumbled
in the dark of my own core calm or turbulent,

this invitation
to dive with you into this current this oceanic wave
to share in ways warm, sincere, caring, powerful,
palpable, defined, precise, definitive, so sure, specific,
articulate, unhesitating, unambiguous, so enticing, intense,

until there is this deep penetrating satiation
fulfillment soul intimacy
that is our most complete nourishment.

As I wish and dream that I might bless you,
you indeed most surely bless me.

III. Through the Faces of Rage

When we are struggling

When we are struggling, when life is not easy,
the desire for love and human closeness
may come upon us.

In a Poetic Image
Love pushes us to new heights.
It brings us
   to recognize the tension
   between our hopes and wishes,
   and the way things actually are.
We can taste the disappointment ~
   a bittersweet yearning for connection
   not yet fulfilled.
Let's not create defeat, go off into cold
   indifference,
   disconnection,
   isolation.
Even less so into harsh
   insulting,
   threatening,
   rage,
   violence.
May we have the courage,
   the inspired energy,
   to go through
   what we must
   to come to feel
   whole and safe, vibrant and alive,
   where human contact and warmth
   allow for deep
   soulful connection.

Harassed

Feeling attacked by criticism or threats
thrown at us in harsh anger, our reactions can be
fear, hurt, irritation, aggression in reply.

Even staying with our own feelings,
when we feel disturbed,
sensing that we are suffering without a cause,
not replying in anger
but believing the attacks to come
from a disturbed distorted viewpoint,
here too we still stay in reactivity,
still reside in our righteousness.

Having gone beyond our own aggressive reactivity,
we now stay with our own reactive torment.

To leap the gap from us to the other, these steps:

while seeing our reaction to the other's anger that
comes at us, not staying in our reaction, this time,

going back through our reaction,
going through the other's anger,

coming to see
the other's pain and unfulfilled needs
inspiring that anger.

And yet, that pain, those needs,
reflected in the intensity of the attack on us,
may themselves be too turbulent for us.
And we are not invited to see them,
given the expression of anger, hiding pain or needs.

We might then stay with anger flying back and forth,
or with our own distress, righteously ineffective,
sadly having no realization of,
and so showing no recognition of,
the other's tormented pain and needs.

Shame swirling into viciousness

Shame drowning me
my deepest essence
so ugly and horrible
needing to keep myself
hidden forever and ever.

I find myself without thought
acting without understanding
fighting to avoid this shame somehow
somehow
following the urge to do something however bizarre
however rough or random.

Wait! They ask what's happening. Don't they see it?
That's it! They don't see the source of my limitless
fountain of shame! Quick! I'm brilliant!
How can I hide it then from everyone else?

Mine's perhaps a rare case, most assuredly a special case.
I see now the brilliant creativity of my inspired action plan.
My genius inventiveness in action, dissimulating!
The inspired singularly masterly method in my madness!

Swirling spinning dizzy
in anguish
I thrash about madly
attacking and hurting to show my toughness.
The more injuries, harm, fear to others
all the better
to feel guilt at my actions ∼

When I look at my actions, I can avoid seeing myself.

D o i n g horrible things
is much more easy to live with
than *b e i n g* horrible.

Why are you yelling at me?

Why are you yelling at me?
I'm not deaf.

When you yell something at me, whatever it is,
it is hard for me to hear what it is that you are saying ～
mostly I hear only your yelling.

If you are frustrated,
please let me know what you are frustrated about,
how I might help you in your frustration.
Still, I do not want to be attacked,
do not want you
to fling your frustration on me,
to use me as your whipping boy.

When you insult me,
are condescending to me,
act disgusted by me,
I feel neither your love nor your caring for me.
Nor your respect for me.

And it is just about impossible for me
to feel love and respect for you
when you are acting those ways.
So neither of us wins in that situation,
so far as I can tell.

You do make me wonder about you,
about how you are seeing the situation,
oh you make me want to ask you straight out:

Do you think that I enjoy being
the target of your frustration,
even when not
the reason you are frustrated?

Do you think you are attractive
when you act this way?

Do you think I deserve such a harsh treatment?

Do you want my love in this?
Do you at least want my presence? Want me
not to leave you in a flurry? If so,
is this the most effective way
to get these from another person?

If you are yelling at me
in the hopes of inspiring me
to act in a more mature
grounded
calm
clear-minded way,
that is a painfully inefficient
means to achieve such a goal.
Your yelling only leads me to be
uncomfortable
frightened
angry.

And then I want no contact with you,
period, full stop.
We both end up losing.
How might this be transformed
so we both win?

Between insult and counter-attack

When we are insulted or attacked
in words or deeds
or accused
especially with lies,
our first urge may be
> to counter-attack
> to correct justify explain ourselves
> to run away
> or
> to act as if nothing were amiss.

Each of these has its benefits
and each, its incompleteness.

The issue is not addressed and resolved,
but intensified, avoided, or ignored.

The situation begs for resolution
and a sense of being finished.

Few can respond to the issue
simply
resolutely
calling a spade a spade
describing things as they are
in ways that touch the core of the situation.
Few speak as did
Joseph Welch to Joseph McCarthy, declaring clearly
(U.S. Senate Subcommittee Hearing, June 9, 1954),
> "Until this moment, Senator,
>   I think I never really gauged
>   your cruelty or your recklessness,"
and, after more barbed discussion, continuing,
> "You have done enough.
>   Have you no sense of decency, sir, at long last?
>   Have you left no sense of decency?"

Waltzing around pain

We learn to dance,
to waltz around pain,
from the British stiff upper lip
through "Yo, bro" and "Hola, chico" macho greetings
and gangland tough-guy looking-for-a-fight poses
to the Far East ethics of expressionless saving face.

We learn to hide, to suppress pain, and we learn
not to recognize, not to acknowledge, another's pain.
We don't want to make
their task of not facing their anguish
any harder, do we?
That's only being kind (albeit blind).

We bump and boogie our way through hard rock rage,
putting our moves on one another
as if this harshness were satisfying.

Our pain is disguised as explosive anger, insults, threats.

These are dance leads that
invite following in the same tempo ∼
counter-malignments, threats, enraged curses.
Everyone getting down,
doing the mutual strangle-hold mambo, getting high
on self-righteous variations
on the You've Hurt Me So Much rhapsody.

Patiently waiting, internal rhythms of deep sadness
subtly request transcription into minor-key blues,
where tenderness comes in
with swaying melodies, warm healing harmonies,
inviting the dancers' embrace ∼
an alternate final slow dance to close the show,
able to bestow tender, respectful connection
beyond conventions of toughness.

How powerful thoughts are

How powerful thoughts are
can be appreciated whenever
we notice how we are pushed along
in torrents of ideas and images
that present themselves with such force
and clarity and intensity

that we do not question them at all
but take them to be undeniably
true, significant, important,
even defining of our world.

Here we have lost a sense
of stillness and of peace,
a sense of context, situation, limitation.
Present are intense judgments and urges
pushing us to act immediately,
perhaps declaring these
momentary impulses as
eternal absolute truths.
The driving force may be fear,
anger, hurt, or repulsion,
it may be exuberant joyous mania,
or utter spinning confusion.

This is a torrent of mind
best to watch from the shoreline
until it subsides, a time to
take a breath (or a thousand) and
pause, watching mind and body
until calm groundedness and ease return.

Where did that thought come from?

Where did that thought come from?
is a question we ask ourselves
from time to time,
when surprised by it
or when practicing tracking thoughts
back to their origins
in the immediate context
or to their more distant roots and
visionary aims.

Where does that thought go?
What is its point?
What will it encourage me to feel?
Does it lead to inspiration?
To a feeling of being attacked unjustly,
a mistreated victim to be pitied and helped?
To annoyance? Hurt? A sense of
power? A sense of rejection?
Does it lead to good will?
To anger? To fear? To shame?
Does it open me to the world?
Shut me off? Or shut out the world?

What has not yet happened
can in this way be appreciated now
before we are led there.
We may want to take another path,
guide ourselves into another direction,
not taking that particular thought
as a guiding Polar Star.

Shame closing or opening

Your slightest glance bores harshly through me.
I want to hide, to disappear,
to be invisible, to be non-existent.

I want to lash out at myself before you will,
before others will.
I feel worthless, disgusting, dirty.
I feel it was a mistake that I was born,
a mistake that I am still alive.
I feel I am a curse to the world, and am cursed.

If you pretend that you do not notice me,
this is for the best
(I declare
in an unconvincing voice).
If you pretend to respect me ∼
and in that you must certainly be pretending (I am
too low to be respected in any way) ∼
you only doubly insult me.

Shame is not easy for me but it is more than I deserve.

Despite this,
I see how important
it is to me
how you think of me.

So let me turn back to the source,
to the situation, to see
how in fact you do,
instead of closing my eyes
and mind
and assuming the worst.

Guilt

Your sideways glances accuse me of misdeeds.
I know what you're thinking about!

You know very well why I did what I did,
said what I said.

It's all because of you and you know who!
If any of you bother me any more, you'll regret it.
Leave me alone!

You started it all.
I was just protecting what was mine to protect.

If you think this is harsh, just keep it up
and boy, will you see what I am capable of!
And it isn't pretty!

I didn't do anything!

So what's that that I hear you mumbling about?

Oh. Somehow here I hear you as clear as my own voice.

I can see now! Yes, despite my denials,
counter-attacking criticisms, and threats,
my deeper sense (I am ashamed to admit your point),
my dear oh my dear,
yes, I will speak it out, I do certainly see
that I have hurt someone knowingly, or unintentionally.

Please, then, let me show you I know your hurt, at least,
and so open the door to apologies or compensation,
helping you directly,
correcting for my hurting you,
and making revenge unnecessary.

To Hòa thượng (Venerable) Thích Quảng Đức
(born, Hội Khánh, 1897; self-immolated, Saigon, June 11, 1963)

Anger

Anger
is truly a poison.
It destroys our peace
our calm
our open heart.

It feeds on itself
and it feeds on us.
It directs us into violence,
which brings at most
petty, fleeting satisfaction,

candy that seems to feed us
but gives no sense of being nourished.

It then turns against
any sense of lasting satisfying fulfillment
we may feel
from other areas of our life.

It is voracious and insatiable,
firm in a harsh constancy.
Rapacious in its attitude,
it will devour in promiscuous rage

if not overcome for the benefit of
the harmonious well-being
of ourselves and of others
by seeing its roots
and refusing its
narrow, bitter, nasty, driven, malevolent focus.

I bow in respect of those wise,
caring, understanding, grounded, and brave enough
not to be violent against others.

Petty anger

Anger is often
petty, frightened, hiding itself,

unable to face confrontation
yet demanding and threatening,

a petulant child
with no sense of strength
or confidence
throwing spit balls at the teacher's back
then looking skyward
feigning total lack of awareness
all of which manifests in mime
its own fully knowing culpability,

hiding and attacking
while pretending innocence
and non-responsibility,

doing unto others
precisely as it wishes
others would never do to it,

Cowardice playing The Tough Guy,
a role of bravado
a role of belligerency
inviting fear or irritation
and a longing to leave or to fight
a role lacking in elegance
in skillfulness
in grace.

Why, when we want

Why, when we want
love, and recognition, and respect,

do we insult, and
threaten, and
declare a commitment
to reek vengeance

on the very people
we want to
accept us with open arms
and heart?

And why do we thwart our deepest
yearnings and needs
by this hostility
carried out ∼ is it
with full awareness or
with rigid myopia or
with bitter blindness?

Stripped

Stripped
bare of all dignity safety peace.
Hunted trapped dragged.
Forced to serve others.
Used abused violated.
Drained exhausted.
No. Not again. Don't let them.
Oh, why was I born a girl?

I hate myself. I hate you.
I hate everyone. I don't deserve this.

Ah, but I won't be alone in this!
No one will be left out of this.
What I don't deserve,
everyone will know.
No one will be spared.
I pray
that everyone will know my anguish
as I know my anguish,
in my flesh
in my guts,
oh, may everyone know, in theirs.

Bitter wrath, do your work.
Welcome, all, to my hell on earth.
Here I stuff down your throat
a feast of disrespectful insults,
badgering, monstrous, absurd threats,
distorted accusations,
exactly what I've gone through in this hell.

Feel all of that now?
Good! Have I made you feel sympathy for me now?
I hope so. I yearn so. I pray so.

"No sympathy," many answer,
"just nausea, fear, or anger."

My rage

My rage
is frightening me;
I cannot contain it
in my body or mind.
I am going to explode.
I feel dizzy. I feel sick.

Is this normal?

Stop telling me this rage is bad!
I can't be the only one to be feeling this.

Hey! I have a right to feel what I feel. I've got as
good a woman's intuition as anyone I know.
And better even, in fact!
Well, surely you know by now
I can sense how evil and vile you are.
You others,
do you think you can fool me
pretending to be nice, to be caring?
I'm no fool! I'll rip off your mask.
When I get you to burst out with
more rage than even I feel,
I can convince myself
I am perfectly OK.
You fakes!

But wait, what's this?
Oh! Do I *ever* need you here! I hate you!

My desperate need for you nauseates me.

Women and men of rage, unite!

Calling all men of rage, all women of rage.

Let's not commit ourselves
to a Rageholics Anonymous
self-flagellating repentance!
Rather, let's look at our rage,
let's not deny it
but
let's not hurt or destroy
with it, either.

Let's each learn our own path in,
in to our heart-most interior,
to know what is going on
to become clear about what
our true, primary frustrations are
so we do not waste time
being lost
exploding here and there
wherever the least irritant is felt,
the least obstacle encountered.

Let's be done finally with
this cycle of violence
we are all all-too-familiar with.

In the cards

What's in the cards?
A conventional cant has it
that we do not control
the cards we are dealt
but do control
how we play these cards.

When we find ourselves confronted
by an invitation
to respond in kind
to an insult or a threat

how do we keep sane
and true to our own values?

How do we deal with,
respond to,
such aggression,
without becoming rage-filled and myopic
ourselves?

If we slow it down, keep from a knee-jerk reactivity,
we can see the invitation
but keep a larger
sense of reality,
containing the invitation
but not being cramped into its confines.

The challenge to go deeper

The challenge to go deeper
than accepting the invitation to stay
on the turbulent surface

when insults
invite insults,
when false, distorted accusations
invite aggressive counter-attacks,

how can we respond to this request
that we stay in a fight mode?

How can we deal with it adequately, fully,
as is nonetheless called for,
and yet experience and express
a fuller grounding,
a larger context,
a vision that is
not based on rage?

Beyond vengefulness

Vengefulness may be dismantled,
undone, finished with.
>*It's not that simple*
>*but it's not that complex.*

Its two parts are distinct.
Do not confuse the two.
>*It's not that simple*
>*but it's not that complex.*

Its first part is ill-willed, malevolent, malicious, vicious.
Second is its dress of righteousness, defining
us as addressing wrongs done to us,
as administering justice.
>*It's not that simple*
>*but it's not that complex.*

First, strip the maliciousness to its naked ugliness.
Make amends, stop ongoing insults, lies, threats,
recant public defamations, slander, harassment ∼
apologize.
>*It's not that simple*
>*but it's not that complex.*

Investigate the anger and its root source
of feeling violated, not in instances
here and now letting us see our tender
spots and issues (our buttons so easily
pushed) but in the real times
now long gone the times that ∼
festering wounds that they are ∼ still hurt.
After years of delay here,
go back to the source.
Deal with it directly.
Stop distracting from the real work to be done
within.
>*It's not that simple*
>*but it's not that complex.*

Do not confuse the two parts.
Each has its own treatment,
its own resolution.
>*It's not that simple*
>*but it's not that complex.*

Our anger in its impotence and beyond

Our anger in its impotence
Leaves in limbo our frustrated longings,
          our desires not yet satisfied.

Our first frustration,
another's disrespectful disregard
of who we are, of what we want.

Then, our second,
our losing sight of those still frustrated longings
(still alive and now ready to fester)
as we refocus on punishing the other.

A fatal frustrating shift and distorting distraction.

Beyond this distorted stance,
this vengefulness ～
          it's not that simple
          but it's not that complex ～
we can perhaps return to appreciate
our longings,
seeing their insignificance and letting it be,
not worth a struggle or our worry,
or, another sense of what touches us,
seeing their value in our lives
and returning to search for their
satisfaction and ours,
and a completion and a peace.

I get you to be angry

I get you to be angry
or I get myself to see you
as harsh and unfair

so that I can encourage and demand
caring, gentle compassion, which
I never had when I needed it.

But if you give it to me
I know this has no value

because it means you weren't
truly enraged at me
the way I need it to be
in order for your compassion to
mean I have finally
received it now as I have needed it
for so many years.

I explode in rage or melt in exhaustion and frustration.

Shame

Shame that burns through
to the heart

intense shame so intense
she would sooner choose nothing,
would sooner choose death.

She cannot convince
herself of her right to live.

Thinking has no power here.

Her dry inner well needs filling
here with other than ideas.

She needs to be held
to be loved
to be rocked gently
a lullaby sung
against her body
its resonant vibrations
warming her soul
and giving her strength
to carry on
in that all-embracing love.

Ignorance

Ignorance
in one understanding of the idea
is most powerful
when it is not simply
a lack of knowledge

but false assumptions
parading
as if importantly true.

When we sense ourselves
to be driven
or enraged
or find ourselves to be self-righteous

or when we repeat an action
that refuses to achieve
its envisioned goal,
the goal we long for
and demand, are certain we deserve,
and that we
envision to be its certain outcome

that is when we may be dragged
along by just this
pompous parading ignorance.

"Tell me about your relationship to pain, and I will tell you who
you are!"
Ernst Jünger (1895-1998), "Über den Schmerz," in *Blätter und Steine*
(1934), pp. 154-213, translated from text at p. 155; essay reprinted in
Sämtliche Werke, vol. 7 (1980), pp. 143-191, with text at p. 145.

Bitterness

We all know pain; some know bitterness
as well.
How is this?
If we find bitterness,
what is possible now for us?
Are we stuck forever,
doomed to torment ourselves and others?

Bitterness can blind us
to the pain of others
while it serves its key function
of distracting us from our own
sense of being hurt, betrayed, and defenseless,
giving us
an empty sense of power
built of others' torment.

Here others see us as despicable tyrants.

And we can all see our own hard-heartedness,
which cramps and crimps our ability
to appreciate the successes and happinesses of others,
and blocks our sense of simple joy at life's wonders.

The absurdity of ridicule

Hobbling through the streets of Tangiers,
supported by two crutches,
my foot and its three fractured bones
in a cast still hardening,
I am being mocked by a man sitting on
the ground, taking
a break from begging,
to point a long bony finger
in my direction, and to
screech out a biting laugh,
staring at me with
his one remaining eye.
A tormented man's moment of terrible mirth.

A fish flails about

Bait bitten
a fish flails about
hung in the air
fishhook its fate
no water to breathe
asphyxiated.

A dog wounded
then approached
growls and bites
in useless defense
against its pain.

Words ripping
into old wounds ~
time to lick and soothe,
to take a breath,
but rage stops all healing,
the bait bitten and eaten whole ~
a vicious dance
of bloody partners
dressed in bitterness.

The end ~
dancers collapse,
one walks away,
a call for gentleness finds an ear,
or the music ends,
soon to start anew.

You invite me into a pit

You invite me into a pit
muck-thick in false
accusations
you have put forth,
dressing yourself
as an unjustly treated victim,
creating out of nothing
a dramatic story
of your righteousness.
Any questioning of your
nasty creative
fable
upsets you,
all taken by you as further injustice.
Digging yourself
deeper into
a self-defensive
hole while
slashing out insults
a last time
before covering yourself
in a flag of the paired stripes
of crusader rabbit and holy martyr.

A most dark enigma

Though I have tried
to fathom your depths
for so many moons
I never reach a sense of
what pains you
behind the pains
you present as façade so
lifeless and rigid
as recited story
trotted out in ritualistic recitation,
as impenetrable curtain
refusing to reveal,
it begs being lifted
to present a tender caring
soul.
Fearing the worst,
not realizing the promise
of warm human contact,
it remains turbulently
unhealed.

Gandhi would have turned over in his grave

If he had been buried ∼
and not cremated
in traditional Hindu ceremony ∼
Gandhi would have turned over in his grave
if he saw the way some
apply his teachings,
for him to see his respect for harmlessness,
ahimsa,
and his principle of holding on to the truth,
satya-graha,
cited as catch phrases
by those who go on to
destroy the difference
between truth and distortion,
throwing in total fabrications out
of the air (out of an imagination
stewing in rancor, in vengefulness),
in the service of bitter
vilification and the gratuitous
destruction of others' well-being.

We're angry

We're angry
at others now for
how we fear we might become,
or sense vaguely, or clearly,
that we once were.

We see all of the torment, the dukkha,
our worries about who we really are lead to.
Attempts at self-definition too are
passing mental processes,
arising out of specific particulars, this or that.
No reason to clutch on to these attempts,
these patterns.
We let go; we let them go by.
No self; no worry about self-image.

Self-image: mirage of a delusion.

No self-image;
no fears, worries, anxieties about who we are.

Time to end self-doubt is
when the issue of self and self-definition
or essential nature arises,
whenever it arises,
then and there.

Seeking compassion

Seeking compassion
we display our pain, our sadness,
awakening our tender underbelly ∼
a time to focus attention on our mind's still-point,
within, to sense and to intensify our inner stability.

Now, to inspire compassion, a soulful mix:
a goodly portion of strong and pliant
courage of the heart needing no defense,
to invite the expression of human warmth,
and a healthy dollop of pliant and strong
openness to allow in this soothing tenderness.
With this, compassion that is offered
can enter within, can permeate throughout
in its reassuring ways, nourishing us in our depths,
offering us this portal to profound refuge
vibrant relaxed grounding through heart-felt connection.

Our tender sadness wisely dressed in peaceful welcome,
we encourage gentle caring to be extended
in reverence to us.

Strong and soft in this inner bravery,
we are honored and cared for, our isolation overcome.
To everyone's benefit.

Unless worried weakness
demands us to stand defended as a fortress,
has us cowardly desert
our soft soulful search for compassion,
has us feign a Tough As Nails façade,
fooling others and perhaps ∼ even worse ∼
ourselves, and has us howl, growl, bare teeth, snap, bite
at any who would approach, barking out to one and to all,
Stay away! Beware! Mad dog!

Then, strong and aggressive in inner fear,
our isolation intensified, we receive no compassion.
To everyone's loss.

Violence against children

We are all largely incompetent,
incapable of wise understanding and elegant action,
omnipotent only in our most exaggerated dreams,
largely powerless in the face of the forces
that guide our health, life course, destiny, death.
We take these limitations this inelegance
these clumsy unseeing distorted views
into all situations, all relationships, in our life.

So naturally when it comes to raising children,
we take our confused understandings
of how we think, react, judge, misread others,
seeing in our discomfort confusion irritation frustration
a child in need of reprimanding scolding beating and
in our attraction yearning powerful urges for satisfaction
we see a child as teasing testing tempting dirty
inviting us to that marriage of lust and disgust
that is the hallmark of the violent pornographic mind
distortingly seen as the child's.

Such dangerous incapacities we can bring with us!

Slipping into moral judgments

Slipping into moral judgments
about how he presents himself to her,
how his aggressive actions are aimed at
insulting her, hurting her,
she loses sight of
the human struggle
to make life bearable
that he presents to her eyes, right in front of her.
Now blinded,
she bites the hook ∼ his rage at first, not hers ∼
inviting her to join in,
and, blindly, she does ∼ with her rage now, not his.

Becoming faint at it all, too much for her,
her heart is heavy
in sadness and rage she cannot accept.

All this from blindness of another's driven anguish.
This is not a gift to herself or to him.
Both lose in this story.

"This ... represents a small measure of justice in this heartless world."
Szmuel Lajb Sznajderman, known as S. L. Shneiderman (1906-1996), "Light in the Darkness," in *Between Fear and Hope* (1947), p. 229.

The shrapnel of my rage

People yearn for fairness justice gentle respect
with a yearning suppressible but not destructible
even by governmental use of brute military police force.

The shrapnel of my rage
rips through my heart
splays forth
        not caring
        who is innocent
        who is powerless.
        (The enemy and our most belovèd
        are equally harmed in this violence.)

Blood from my entrails
screams
for revenge ∼ seed to more torment and revenge ∼
for justice
for peace,
for love.

Deep confusions and agitations rule in this rage.

What's so hard about apologizing?

Apologizing is a gift
we give to another
that allows both of us to come to peace.
Yet some people seem deathly allergic to apologizing.

To refuse to apologize keeps our self-image pure,
allows us to tell ourselves that we have never ever
done anything wrong or hurtful or hurting.

With that, we blind ourselves to
our actions that ended up hurting
or causing problems for another,
to our actions that had that design
or that unexpected consequence.

An apology is a salve for healing.

What's so hard about expressing thanks?

Thanking someone is a gift
that shows our appreciation
for another's contribution to our lives,
gives to the other a sense of worth and recognition.
Yet some people seem deathly allergic to thanking another.

To refuse to give thanks keeps our self-image independent,
allows us to tell ourselves that we don't need anybody
for anything; keeps our self-image strong, helps us feel
invulnerable, or at least a little less vulnerable.

With that we blind ourselves to
the joy of warm, intimate connection with another person,
to a sense of the way we can each be of great value
in the lives of one another.

Giving thanks is a lubricant for friendship.

I apologize for it all, after it all

I apologize for it all, after it all,
for what I have done and have not done,
for everything that was done or not done.
For an inability to eliminate violence and killing,
for wars and hatreds everywhere,
for a world that cannot live in harmony,
in mutual caring,
or even merely in mutual respect,
in civility.
I apologize for a world that is far from loving.
*(If I were indeed all-mighty, all-seeing, all-comprehending,
I would feel painfully ashamed of myself.)*

To you,
I apologize for everything that brought you misery.
I apologize for not being there in your childhood
when you relied on someone to protect you
who did not ~
a frightened or frustrated mother, a needy or raging
father, uncle, brother,
a confused neighbor who could not see, or wouldn't,
a friendly but untrustworthy stranger ~
for not protecting you from these and from others,
from their betrayal
of your body, mind, heart, soul.

I apologize for not being there to celebrate your successes.
For not being there to help in your times of sickness,
of aging, of mortal trembling facing death.

I apologize for your haunting, relentless memories,
harsh with swirling hatreds
(another's? yours? a broth of both?),
for the tormented explosions of those whirlwinds
directed outwards against others,
for a world you saw
as dangerous,
as treacherous with its deceiving deceptions,
for a world

that inspired
a virulent vigilance and an exciting urge
to plot destruction of threats you felt,
for insincerities, breeding ground of betrayals, and,
born of those wounds,
your lack of security that would allow an open heart.

I apologize that we live in such a world.

If you could go back there,
so long ago, a lifetime ago,
and recognize how innocent you were,
how harsh the world was,
how abandoned you felt,
and together with that
appreciate here
that despite that, because of that,
others now can feel deep sadness at your pain,

then a double opening would be possible:
 a cleansing incision offering drainage, healing,
 and a door offering new pathways, new promise.

I apologize for not being there for you ～
for not knowing
how to get through to you helpfully,
how to bring to you
a caring approach you could recognize
in your heart and guts, unquestionably.

These apologies
invite sharing a heartfelt awareness of sadness
 and the healing born of recognition.

"... when someone does not manage to live, because a domestic tyrant forbids his development, because a religion fetters his flourishing, because a culture numbs his spirit, because misery prevents him from living, because an army of occupation destroys all cultural organization, in such an impoverished environment, the spell of terrorism offers a moment of existence, a spurt of dignity.
Boris Cyrulnik (1937-), *Autobiographie d'un épouvantail* (2010), translated from the text at p. 106.

Private problems, group aggression

Alone with my torments
my stresses confusions yearnings,
searching for meaning, for a place in the world,
drawn to others
rebels with a cause
or so they seem,
drawn to others
soon to be my brothers, my family.

I join the group, learn the talk,
practice the rituals,
focus on the task at hand: group aggression ∼
rebellion on a grand scale
violence to shake the world
urban warfare.

All those not with us: targets (guilty and sinful).
All traitors ready to find peace with our enemies: targets.
All seeming innocents: targets.
All critics of our truths: targets.
We have no shortage of targets.

Their losses, our celebrations.
At last I am at home.
Home, our home, bloody home, but my home.

IV. Faces of War

"War plays havoc with the refinements of conscience."
British Prime Minister (1916-1922) David Lloyd George (1863-1945),
The Truth about The Peace Treaties, vol. 2 (1938), p. 765.

The realities of war

Wars offer us retrospective options.

We can forget them.

We can glorify them in sanitized
heroic myth
swaddled in flags, clothed in splendid uniforms,
to the tune of triumphant military marches.

We can remember them
as organized violence
benefitting some in hiding, directing
unseen back-stage,
and benefitting in a grander, more ethereal way,
others proud of their nation's prowess and right,
each war marking its generations with grief,
mourning, a memory for revenge,
disrupting peace
creating countless tragedies,
personal and societal.

Defensive wars

Once upon a time kings
led their forces out
into the fields to meet
other kings with *their* forces,
leaving peasants to carry on
growing crops, needed for whoever survived.
But that was a then now gone.

Now wars are different now war is held to be justified
          if another country attacks first or
              if its troops gather on our border threateningly.
That's called a defensive war.

For having directed a non-defensive war, an offensive war,
after due convictions in the Nuremberg trials,
key leaders of the Third Reich went to the gallows.

This attitude and legal idea (precedent) led nations
around the globe to redefine their War Departments
as Departments of Defense, at least a renaming ritual.

But this too is perhaps merely one more outmoded idea
we can forget about now, on our way
to uncivilized extinction.

Might does not make wrong right.
Perhaps, rather, might makes right wrong.

Do we join this devolution?
This dive into rule by power?
Or shall we play penny ante poker as
our global *Titanic* sinks below the waves?

Can we learn once again
to keep on breathing free of hatred
in peace and radiant love?

"Our Armies, as all armies ... were schools of slaughter."
Sir Philip Gibbs (1877-1962), *Realities of War* (1920), p. 450.

The sands

The sands
drink in
our blood
their blood
your blood.
They shed no tears
they have no stake here
and so
easily
absorb it all, endlessly,
the mystery of senseless violence
being written in the sands,
and yet,
and yet
we
stand firm with beliefs
and visions
knowing right from wrong
and even (so we will whisper,
with eyes humbled,
or shout to the heavens)
righteousness from evil.

The dead and maimed and widowed and orphaned
are not impressed.

On the horizon wait jackals
in the pious garb
of many nations.

"Direct losses, that is, those which are caused by direct acts of war, can occur both in the military as well as among the civilian population." ... "Civilian losses from hostilities are not limited to the victims of aerial bombing and shelling."
Boris Urlanis (1906-1981), *Bilanz der Kriege. Die Menschenverluste Europas vom 17. Jahrhundert bis zur Gegenwart* (1965), translated from text at p. 14, and Boris Urlanis, *Wars and Population* (1971), p. 20.

Hiding, denying, disregarding the toll of war

War dead: why a number so difficult to determine?
Information is filtered (for national security, they say),
while we hear of the enemy's lying distortions, absurd
propaganda, and revolting war crimes. And of *their* dead.

Military censorship: a vital mission for national survival.
He who recounts it, controls and defines the story.

No talk is the best course of censorship.
Next, talk of the enemy's losses, precise, maximized.
If need be, talk of our military losses, vague, minimized.

Losses ⁓ what is counted here? who is counted?
He who counts, controls and defines the story.

Easiest to identify are military dead, killed in action,
including killed by our own forces, friendly fire,
as if that made it more pleasant or agreeable.
Add those who die somewhat later from wounds,
or from other complications, limited to military personnel
in the area of violence and combat, the theater of war.
Then, add those who are counted as not traceable,
as missing in action (until time makes the question moot).
Next, servicemen held prisoner in camps, who die
at some often ill-defined time, in unstated conditions,
and those sick to death, perhaps in epidemic proportions.

On another level of consideration or inclusiveness,
usually in later decades (or centuries),
list those from the military whose lives
are finished forever,

but who live on, crippled, maimed, or with spirit killed ∼
these ex military men sometimes simply dismissed
as cowards, deserters, traitors to the cause, to the nation,
or, if declaring war to be the greatest of crimes, psychotics.

Usually there is no counting in of innocents, civilian
victims of guns, cannons, explosives, bombs, missiles,
caught between two armies, caught in crossfire,
in jargon, collateral damage from military hardware.

For a comprehensive overview, often not wanted,
easiest overall count is population before the war
minus population after the war, for those who died.
But what of those unborn, those who emigrated,
those who immigrated to fill the labor gap, what of the
national tendencies of population change (often growth)
through the years up to the start of hostilities
(often shrinking starting from that point in time)?

Nor do we count
the number of family and friends now in mourning,
devastated, discouraged, lost.
Nor those blinded in battle, amputees, basket cases.
Nor those who would never have a family,
future generations never to be born,
as seen reflected in statistics, in lower birth rates ∼
another direct impact on population.
And a generation later,
another wave of fewer new marriages, fewer children.

Nor the impact of war's destruction
on the nation's physical conditions, its exhaustion,
its instability, its need for reconstruction, for recovery,
its resources redirected from deeper national purposes.

Although definitely recited in many families' stories,
officially most of these specifics are often omitted,
distorting the full impact of war on people and the society.

Tormented memories and tempestuous events
r e v e r b e r a t i n g   t h r o u g h   t i m e .

"… the glory of the soldier is a lie, like everything in war that has the air of being beautiful."
Henri Barbusse (1873-1935), *Le feu* (1916), Chap. XXIV; translated from text in editions of 1916 (p. 376), 1965 (p. 433), and 2010 (p. 374).

*Among **young men not** surviving the Great War (1914-1918), the noble War to End All Wars, were 32.2% of **all** German men aged 21-26 when the war began, 24.5% of **all** Frenchmen 17-20, & 16.2% of **all** British men 23-27! Leaving aside misery & mourning, hunger, famine, & starvation, orphans, widows, & mutilated veterans, momentous epidemics & horrendous genocidal massacres, estimates of **total** war dead range upwards from 8.5 million military & 6.5 million civilians (non-combatants, but still ending up quite dead) ~ all solemn tributes to the terrifying gravity of war.*

J'ai le cœur déchiré

J'ai le cœur déchiré
par ces guerres qui s'écoulent infiniment,
par cette violence des gouvernements acharnés,
par ces viols des faibles par des puissants impotents.
Je suis écœuré par ces grands mots inspirés
qui font couler du sang
et briser les vies des pauvres gens.

> My heart is torn to shreds
> by endless wars,
> the violence of governments and desperate leaders,
> rapes of the weak by the impotently powerful.
> I am disgusted by justifications
> that let blood flow,
> that shatter the lives
> of so many poor souls and entire countries.

See here Michel Huber, *La Population de la France pendant la guerre* (1931), Rudolf Meerwarth, *Die Einwirkung des Krieges auf Bevölkerungsbewegung, Einkommen und Lebenshaltung in Deutschland* (1932), Boris Urlanis, *Wars and Population* (1971), J.M. Winter, *The Great War and the British People* (1985), Adam Hochschild, *To End All Wars: A Story of Loyalty and Rebellion, 1914-1918* (2011), etc. In fiction, see here Henri Barbusse, *Under Fire [Le Feu]* (1916), *The War Poems of Siegfried Sassoon* (1919), Ernst Jünger, *The Storm of Steel [In Stahlgewittern]* (1920), Jaroslav Hašek, *Good Soldier Švejk* (1921-1923), Erich Maria Remarque, *All Quiet on the Western Front [Im Westen nichts Neues]* (1929), Ernest Hemingway, *A Farewell to Arms* (1929), Edlef Köppen, *Higher Command [Heeresbericht]* (1930), etc.

"Old soldiers never die; they simply fide a-why."
Siegfried Sassoon (1886-1967), rendering a certain pronunciation of lyrics sung by British troops in 1916, from "Twelve Months After" (1917), in *The War Poems of Siegfried Sassoon* (1919), at p. 68.

War between the lines

Clichés, military clichés, as significant:
If we think about the meaning of clichés,
what can we learn?
What is their point implications insinuations?

"War is hell."
Hell whatever it is, is not glorious
is not a desirable vacation spot is not a picnic.
The cliché here a counter-balance
to the romanticizing of war.

"Old soldiers never die, they just fade away."
It is not that soldiers are immortal (humans are mortal)
soldiers young and not so young
are surely maimed killed certainly do die.
It is not that old soldiers are super-human.
This fading away happens before death.
From the trip to hell something is left behind
the soldier here less present less solid
less visible faded less vibrant then ultimately
all vibrancy gone faded away fully.

"Lest we forget." and "Never again."
Reminders of something vital,
and something we want to avoid
or want not to repeat.

And yet how varied
the interpretation of what is to be remembered
and what is to be avoided or not repeated.

Behind these and other hopes visions commitments,
deep anguishing pains and torments
remain unmentioned.

"War is a crime against humanity."
In the founding declaration of the group Paco (this name being the
Esperanto word for Peace), 1921, Bilthoven, Netherlands; the group
was later renamed the War Resisters' International or WRI.

Wars start with bellophilia

Wars start
before they start,
with flags and assuredness
of being wronged
or of being in the right, of having the right to fight,
and, even earlier, with children
learning of their duty to do right by their country.

With pomp and ceremony
with great speeches of good and evil ∼
ah, the glory and splendor of it all,
enough to inspire bellophilia in many a heart ∼
and repeated from land to land, from time to time
with stunning consistency,
expressed in the world's tongues, each in its own context.
With stories of heroism, bravery, the evil enemy getting its
due, righteousness triumphing, the world being better.

And those who bear the brunt of this
on the home front with stress and worries and losses
and on the battle front with wounds
and comrades screaming and dying
and orphans and widows and distraught parents
learning of their children dying before their time.

What do these say in their suffering?
Often they speak out loudest for the value of the death,
and the dread that theirs were not killed in vain.
(No one asks what would truly make up for those deaths.)

Afterwards, when peace returns, and these countries,
former enemies, become allies and life (and business)
go on for those who have survived,
what does it all mean in five, fifty, or a hundred years?

"...the nature of Warre ... consisteth not in actual fighting, but in the known disposition thereto, during all the time there is no assurance to the contrary ... consequent to a time of Warre, where every man is Enemy to every man ... In such a condition, there is ... continuall feare, and danger of violent death; And the life of man, solitary, poore, brutish, and short."
Thomas Hobbes (1588-1679), *Leviathan* (1651), Part I, Section 13, Paragraphs 8-9. Original orthography and spelling.

Civil War

War has a stench
that is physical, social, spiritual, metaphysical.
It takes the fabric of society
already always with its tolerable tensions,
transforming them into irreparable violence,
a rape of the society's innocence ∼
if ever it was in that state of simplicity ∼
creating nightmarish moments
burned into our memories.

War when civil, especially, when civil,
sees families split into
enemy camps,
old friends come to be seen as suspicious
or traitorous,
to be hunted down and murdered,
each side feeling righteous, wronged, injured
beyond repair, beyond hope.

Survival becomes a curse.

"The soldier without wounds does not know war."
Gustave Planche (1808-1857), "Histoire et philosophie de l'art. VI: Moralité de la poésie," *Revue des Deux Mondes*, 4th Series, Vol. 1 (1835), pp. 241-263, translated from text at p. 244.

Here I am and the nation honors its war dead

Here I am
in some God-forsaken land
waiting to do right
to give to my country,
ready to die
ready to stay alive
killing if I must.
Who decided this?
Are they here with me
ready to bleed, die, kill?
Or merely ready to toast my bravery with a dry martini?
My comrades, closer than my breath, dying by my side,
calling out for help, for Mommy.
I just want to be remembered
with respect.

So what that the nation honors
its war dead ~
those, as is said, who died fighting
in defense of the nation, to maintain our way of life,
and so forth?
The wishful vow goes forth that they not die in vain!
What? No sadness? No remorse? No apologies?
And what of those who died
years later
sick and penniless, huddled against the elements,
all hopes crushed
in a nation willing to let the sick
die of sickness, the wretched
die in poverty, to let former warriors
beg on the streets,
tasting the glory of the nation in its gutters.

"The word *hero* is so overused. I don't like it… I'm finished with the word *hero*."

Stefan Bałuk (1914-2014), member of the elite British-organized SOE (Special Operations Executive) of Poland's AK (Armia Krajowa, Home Army), in interview with Dave McGuire, "A Polish resistance fighter remembers fighting in the Warsaw Uprising—from the sewers," PBS Radio, *The World*, broadcast October 2, 2014, retrieved that same date from pri.org/stories/2014-10-02/polish-resistance-fighter-remembers-fighting-warsaw-uprising-sewers, at 3m38s-44s, 3m52s-54s in the audio recording; this is also heard in the program presented at rnw.nl/english/article/warsaw-uprising-rebel-fought-nazis-betrayed-communists, in the audio at 12m13s-19s, 12m24s-26s, in "Betrayal" (an episode in the series *This Is The State We're In*, hosted by Jonathan Groubert, for RNI, Radio Netherlands International).

Peace between wars

Peace unto you
And unto you, peace.
May it be.

Blessèd peace, a time of comfort and security,
a time for growth, reflection, warmth, caring,
a time for love and respect, caring and tenderness,
a time for full investigation and appreciation
of all that life can promise.

A time of freedoms that may make some people
nervous, worried, insecure, when people
are enjoying life and not in a state of fear or panic,
    where the teachings of violence will not take root
    with entire peoples directed into murderous self-defense
    quite ready to take "heroic" action
    in order to save all that is seen as threatened.

Fear drives people
more than the urge to natural fulfillment and love,
it would seem.

"But the victors no longer consider themselves bound to the democratic principles proclaimed by them before their success. The ancient brute law of the victor has replaced the promised victory of right."
Foreign Minister Otto Bauer (1881-1938), at the National Constituent Assembly of German Austria, June 7, 1919, as quoted in David Lloyd George, *The Truth about The Peace Treaties*, vol. 2 (1938), p. 944.

It has been said

It has been said
or, at least,
so have I heard,
that we should love our brother as ourselves
that all men are our brethren
that we are all one family
that those who bring peace
are the children of God
are indeed holy, blessèd.
And yet some will take these words
and with a sly twist of idea
and a turning away of heart
declare
that some men are evil
that some are agents of the devil,
or of Satan, of Iblis, of the Anti-Christ,
or of some other, unnamed horrible evil
and so (large leap now!)
we find ourselves
ready and willing
and even eager ∼
if we accept these declarations
and are driven, whether by
fear, sexless power-lust, proud nationalistic inspiration,
promises of future lucre, smug righteousness, or other ∼
to kill (as if magically this does not turn us
into the evil we find nauseating),
to purify our world (pagan sacrifices, these)
with our time-honored ritualized mutual mass murder,
as if the earth had an unquenchable thirst for
human bloodletting.

I think of his earlier tortures

I think of his earlier tortures
under a brutal regime.
My eyes are washed in moisture
I'm cracking up
I'm cracking apart
I'm cracking open
I'm not made for this century
I'll live and I'll die.
And people will love and hate
and be kind and gentle
and mean and violent.
It will not end.
Beyond this lifetime
onwards
the tears (rivers, oceans) will flow
and love fill the heart
(only with this can we live at all).

A parent's torment

In barged the enemy soldiers ∼
rough, stinking, screaming.
I felt hard blows to my head, wounds to my belly,
and fell.
Held down by two of those men,
I heard my family
receive unwelcome
violence against their
bodies and minds.

I was overcome by
my nauseating shame
unable to save them
from this invasion.
Agonized, tormented, I could not faint,
life at times clearly more difficult than death.

I heard enemy laughter
and the warmth of their
spit was on my face as they left
feeling in their bodies
the surging sense of power
over other human beings,
the survivors sadly changed for life.

Soul-rape draped in a flag.

"... hatred gives birth to hatred, and here ... hatred not only poisons, but also stupefies; therefore, guard your communities from being stupefied through hatred."

Nobel Laureate in Literature (1905) Henryk Sienkiewicz (1846-1916), in a letter dated September 7, 1902, to Karol Rose (1863-1940), publisher of the Berlin Polish-language *Dziennik Berliński*, appearing in that paper that September 24th; reprinted in H. Sienkiewicz, *Dzieła: Wydanie zbiorowe*, vol. 53 (1952), pp. 127-134, translated from text at pp. 129, 131.

Daily in times of darkness

Daily in times of darkness,
each and every night,
each and every day,
in moments of strife, and
when hatreds among groups are grown intense,
and wars declared and fought
(as if the usual torments weren't enough!),
what is the perspective we take on it all,
seeing what is on top, the most superficial,
what is submerged, the most subtle?

If we keep alert to it all
(non-ostrich-like),
it is universal caring,
caring for all beings,
wishing all beings well,
that is our natural nobility, our buoy.

"Never was patriot yet, but was a fool."
John Dryden (1631-1700), *Absalom and Achitophel* (1681), line 968.
"Patriotism is the last resort of a scoundrel."
Samuel Johnson (1709-1784), April 7, 1775, as recorded by James
Boswell (1740-1795) in *The Life of Samuel Johnson, Ll.D.*, commonly
referred to as *Boswell's Life of Johnson*, in the entry for that date.

We learn from our elders

We learn from our elders.
We are taught to respect them
to honor them
and much indeed is there to honor and respect
from time to time
from this or that aged source of wisdom.
And yet
we must add
we're sometimes the one-eyed being led by the blind
and those leaders deftly step aside
when the time comes for heroic death.
And so another generation becomes fodder.
We can honor the holiness of peace and the
deep wrong of murder,
those two touchstones of civilization and morality,
but then the flags start to wave
and the battle cry is heard ⌁

    Do not desert your country in its moment of crisis
        (Support the plans for war
        and join the nation's military if
        your blood is young enough) ⌁

then those who call for civilization are quickly
    pushed aside, shut up,
    locked away jailed imprisoned,
    or definitively shipped out deported exiled,
as cowards, as unpatriotic, as traitors.
Or simply killed, quite unceremoniously.

Who is brave enough to endure such epithets
and their wake?

"Members of the German Reichstag! ... Minorities domiciled in Germany are not subject to persecution... Germany has no interests in the West, our fortifications in the West [these being *der Westwall*, the Siegfried Line] are for all times to become the frontier of the Reich... My love of peace and my endless patience must not be mistaken for weakness, much less for cowardice... I will carry on this fight, no matter against whom, until such time as the safety of the Reich and its rights are secured!"
Adolf Hitler (1889-1945), Document No. 471: Speech by the Fuehrer to the Reichstag, September 1, 1939, in *Documents on the Events Preceding the Outbreak of the War. Compiled and published by the German Foreign Office* (New York, 1940, Das Auswärtige Amt ~ The German Foreign Office / German Library of Information), pp. 498-503.

The innocent and the mighty

Even then, statements were honed
for domestic consumption,
where threats pose simply as a plea for justice and honor.

The posturing:

If they would leave us alone and free,
we would all be at peace.
But when they refuse to discuss how to establish fairness
between nations, mutual respect, stable peace,
do they expect us to betray our own countrymen?

Do we want to fight? No.
Do we want peace? Yes.
Do we want justice? Yes, most certainly.

Remarkable! Where are truth and accuracy here?
Governments create self-righteous myths,
glorifying themselves,
denigrating enemies present or future,
and with the waving of their flag
and the trumpeting of martial melodies
neglecting and dismissing
careful investigation and critical judgment,
dishonoring
truth, honesty, decency, security, and nobility.

"If one could go up the Victory Column now, one would hear
Lord God mocking the foolish maliciousness of the earth, which
lives by political parties and perishes by picric acid."
Joseph Roth (1894-1939), "Rundgang um die Siegessäule," *Neue Ber-
liner Zeitung, 12-Uhr-Blatt*, March 15, 1921; translated from article as
printed in *Joseph Roth in Berlin: Ein Lesebuch für Spaziergänger* (1999),
p. 218.

Backroom Tweedledum politics

Political jokes for the apolitical:

A (bad) political joke it is
to be encouraged to *"Get out and vote!"* when
there's only one party, one candidate.

But give us two candidates from two parties
selected in the same unseen backrooms of power ~
twins Tweedledum and Tweedledee (whose positions are
told apart only by those who truly know who's who),
who, as Mother Goose told it,
thrive on their tiring petty bickering
until both are targeted by outside belligerents,
forgetting then their picayune discords
(an outside enemy still the best excuse for unity) ~
and this joke's on us!

From behind the scenes,
pre-trimmed tawdry stories to draw people
into the personal shame of each candidate
by the followers of the other, with all on both sides
so partisan, so loyal and passionate, so righteous!
Crude accusations of the other's self-interested misdeeds,
easy to establish, self-serving interests not scarce
in politicians or other folk, human pettiness and foibles
common as white snowflakes in Siberian winters.

From tenebrous shadows debates arise over titillatingly
insignificant differences in personality, in personal history,
in political positioning. And, new wine in old bottles,
using each nation's historically honored ideals,

visions are presented, fashioned into tunes
the pipers are paid to play, other themes carefully silenced,
artfully directing the public's thoughts and emotions.

Behind the scenes, what is at stake?
*What do we **not** notice, what is **not** mentioned,*
with our attention carefully directed elsewhere?

Unplayed, unquestioned themes stand mute
behind trumpeted tales of national bravado,
of great societal values, the declaring of grand words,
inspiring values (we, hypnotized by paeans to Freedom,
Social Justice, Democracy, Equality, and even Universal
Brotherhood, to Honor of the Nation, Defender of Security,
National Survival, and even Moral Guide to the World),
these petty pretty great noises unrecognized as distraction
from the immorality of violence and the costs of empire,
from one more society without cohesive mutual concern,
driven by private quite unbrotherly desires,
heartlessness reigning,
the nation's wealth drained by those driven
by greed, self-servingly working the system, alone, as
mavericks, or as in packs of wolves. And who wins?

Society, do you, too, win here, or do you, perhaps, lose?

Time for a breath, to pause, to return to our lived reality.
So, to focus on the specific situations of particular people,
who precisely ends up paying what, and how?
What is the cost in wealth and blood we are asked to pay?

When will we appreciate Hobbes, who saw the rent fabric
of society as the seed to civil suspiciousness and violence,
as guarantor for torment, fear, selfish brutishness?

And will we ever understand beyond our society's
paltry dogmas and new-speak jargon?

Fear and greed
    trump
        all human aspirations and compassionate civility.

91

Some "who suffer from certain things cannot remember them except with a horror that paralyzes every other pleasure ..."
Marie-Henri Beyle, known as Stendhal (1783-1842), *Le rouge et le noir* (1830), translated from text in the complete and revised (enlarged) second edition (1862), Vol. 1, Chap. 27, p. 184.

Broken mugs, broken minds

Picric-acid-exploding shells and other creations,
shrapnel missiles, anti-personnel weaponry,
or heavy plumb-lead loads, a thousand kilos heavy,
ah the 1914 to '18 Krupp cannons, huge artillery
sending these missiles forth, at times
from the heavy, stout, and devastatingly potent howitzer
first nicknamed *Dicke Bertha* by German troops,
    then rendered Big Bertha, *Grosse Bertha*, or *Dikke Bertha*,
    after Bertha Krupp, passive proprietress from '02 on
    of Krupp Ironworks ⁓ oh, and recall, too, Berthawerk,
    a Krupp slave camp built in '42 near Auschwitz ⁓
    oh, what a name *that* was,
at times from other, even bigger cannons, cannon fire
crashing down with the force of tons of iron,
splintering and ripping through bodies,
leaving some headless, legless, armless,
leaving others with ripped bellies,
screaming before passing out,
and add to that,
burns from flame throwers, from mustard gas,
with similar weaponry used by the Allies,
each side quick to learn and adopt the enemy's arsenal,
showing the world a new war phenomenon,
the broken faces, broken mugs, broken muzzles,
to render the French phrase *les gueules cassées*
(back in '14 a neologism)
men having lost their jaws, noses,
cheekbones, lips, or foreheads,
but still quite alive, leading to
the inventiveness of Armenia-born Harvard-trained
oral surgeon Varaztad Kazanjian (known in some circles
for creating prostheses for Freud's jaw cancer, in '31) ⁓
wires holding up jaws ⁓ and to still other contraptions,

French reconstructive surgeons inventing away,
in the Parisian Val-de-Grâce Hospital, in Amiens or Lyon,
French medical artists creating masks
held on by straps 'round the head or behind the ears,
offered up on the one side of some battles,
and Krupp engineers, on the other,
offering up steel teeth and steel jaws ⁓
    oh what a war *that* was!

These disfigured or disabled
wounded warriors lived on, crippled or maimed.

And let's not forget those whose lives were finished
forever, but who likewise lived on,
with broken minds, with spirit killed ⁓
often labeled cowards, deserters, or, if so disgusted
by the reality of war daring to declare it to be so,
treated as seriously imbalanced, horribly sick in the mind.

Or, depending on the jargon of the war in question ⁓
new names proliferating as if marking new discoveries ⁓
presumed-knowing psycho-bards create diagnostic rubrics
such as soldier's heart, cannon fever, neurasthenia,
shell fever, or shell shock (with such minor variations as
trench warfare dug-out disease, barbed-wire sickness, and
later, Maginot Line block-house-confined concrete blues),
followed by battle fatigue or combat exhaustion, and then
traumatic war neurosis, PTSD, acute stress disorder,
combat stress reaction, war-zone stress reaction, and so on,
through the wars, the years, the decades, the centuries.

Treatments were a crude Rorschach test reflecting
urgent frustrations and the at-times creative insensitivities
of those treating these troubled souls ⁓
using the cure of electric shock to overcome shell shock
surely cannot qualify as a surreal homeopathic remedy.

All this from a focus on those somehow surviving.
To which we can add the millions cleanly killed in battle.
Who, pray tell, were the lucky, the fortunate in all of this?

Let's get serious

Let's get serious:
We can see the results. We can focus on the results.
We can forget the means.

We may think that the end justifies the means,
that if the end is good
the means are thereby
good, as well, for that consideration alone.

So if you have an ingrown toenail
and it is good for you not to have an ingrown toenail,
one means to that condition is to cut off the toe.
(What? Not offering up your toe?)

We actually judge the means themselves
even if seeing that they lead to something wonderful;
we do not automatically think that the means are good
just because we believe the end result is good.
Unless we start thinking automatically, thoughtlessly.

We may admire a result but find disastrous
the way in which that result was brought about.

When means are horrendous in our eyes,
the desired end may lose all appeal.
We may need to think some more
about what to do and how to do it.
Our laziness and our impatience
and our certainly of the righteousness of our cause
may be dangerous here, pushing us to "go for it"
even without our seeing a way we find palatable or
merely not nauseating.
Sadly, we certainly see this macabre irrational scenario
repeated from country to country, through the centuries.

Descent into civilization

Civilization is our destiny, our future, our promise.
Or so we are taught and have fervently believed.

We think that we have improved over the Dark Ages,
for example, that their barbarity is disgusting, nauseating,
having nothing to do with how we treat fellow humans.

And yet ∼ when we think of the violence and harshness
of those now-long-gone centuries
taken as our measuring rod and then review
the relatively recent past, within reach
of the memory of the oldest among us,
or even stay with our very own present world,
what do we see of contemporary civilized humanity?

We see people able to kill thousands and tens of thousands
of human beings as part of a day's work,
we have seen hundreds of thousands killed or maimed
with one magnificent horrendous bomb or another,
leading to a worldwide storehouse of thousands of bombs
and thousands of rockets for their transportation to target.
Tomás de Torquemada of Castile, of Inquisition fame,
inspired by the methods of Nicolau Eimeric of Catalonia,
compared to our colossal contemporary scale of violence,
tormented relatively few sacred souls.

We see people ready to torture, to assassinate
those disagreeing with their politics, values, theology,
to set off bombs killing people at market, at prayer,
when those targeted belong to another sect,
let alone those committed to another culture or religion.

Prejudice in thought and action are rampant worldwide.
Our civilization marries this to a sophisticated savagery
that knows less and less of a limit,
technological advances leading our civilization down
into dimensions of violence once only present
in mankind's most horrifying, vile nightmares.

A man once

A man once
from Częstochowa
in southern Poland
standing on a railway station platform
Autumn, 1942
(the German-created ghettos already
being efficiently emptied out)
offered a guard
his elegant coat
in exchange for the guard's agreement
to turn his back
while wife and daughter
slid down an embankment
to hide, to escape, to survive.
To his wife's concern
about his freezing without a coat
that coming winter,
his grandson told me, decades later,
he reassured her
that where he was going
he would have
no need of a coat.

A man once
began a voyage,
not to nearby Auschwitz,
but north beyond Warsaw,
to unmarked train-destination
dedicated extermination camp
Treblinka.

The man was correct about the coat.

V. There is a Goodness

There is a goodness

There is a goodness,
a goodness so sweet
that when we taste it
we cannot stop tears
that come in our joy.

A goodness that draws us to it
without any demand or directions.
We are drawn
as thirsty deer to mountain streams,
as serious scholars to thick tomes,
to this source of nourishment, of inspiration,
instinctively, refreshingly, beautifully,
joyfully, easily, naturally.

It is a gentle, undemanding caring
a love for us and for all at the same time
a love making us feel special and at the same
intensely human, like all of humanity.

When we are in the company of such a caring,
we sense we are in the presence of something, someone
so special we have no name here ∼
do we speak of a saint or of a holy person?
speak of an enlightened being or of a gift to humankind?

We may even see that we could have this same
frame of heart
frame of mind.

Do we dare become what we can imagine is
possible for us and the world?

*Dare we give
merely one drop of our love to see the way it is absorbed
by the world?*

My father's prayer

My earthly father
who art gone from earth
who are gone now
far from here
your absence is great
it is overwhelming
a chasm between you and me
I cannot cross.
And yet who is closer
to my jugular at this moment?
You are a bubbling spring
able to quench a deep longing
in my heart,
if you are willing in my mind
and I am welcoming in my heart.
You are the greatest
of contradictions and yet so real,
as reverberations of your memory
resonate to my deepest depths.

In a moment of impasse

The challenge of climbing the vertical wall
out of early violence-hurts
(at a moment of impasse).

What could be the simplest of tasks
is sometimes overwhelming.

Too weak today to rise
above this reactive
nasty condescending
mind
and its high-pressure
means of
constricting
the caring heart.

This is a time for quiet,
to keep from hurting
all those around us.

She looks out into the world

She looks out into the world
and is struck by what is unfair, unjust, unkind.
And here and there,
she sees some of what she herself has done or thought,
feels ashamed, is afraid others will see these same faults
in her as she can now see out there in others.

The simple thing would be to come
to resolution about this,
to accept this possibility (this remembered past history)
and get on with helping those in torment.

But no! What is simple is too difficult here.
So she is in hiding from her own seeing awareness
of a past she is still agitated about,
worried recognizing that she too
could have been or actually has been
the very person she is now criticizing, afraid
that she will be pointed out and ridiculed or attacked.
Here is the legacy of guilt.

This makes it harder for her to feel right in criticizing,
makes it harder for her to stand up for those in dire need,
those whose plight touches her deeply,
makes it harder for her to be fully human.

First then putting shame and guilt into context,
seeing with sympathetic understanding
   the needs she sensed so demanding so vital,
   the goals she sought so specific so urgent,
   the means employed so unhelpful so limited,
   the actions performed so unskillful so cruel.

This humble tender remorseful sadness
is mother of a sense of a more caring humanity,
an inspiration for helping the world be less harsh.

"My Freinds ... I desire ... with your Love and Consent, that we may always live together as Neighbours and freinds, else what would the great God say to us, who hath made us not to devoure and destroy one an other but live Soberly and kindly together in the world ... I have great love and regard towards you, and I desire to Winn and gain your Love & freindship by a kind, just and peaceable life; and the People I send are of the same mind, & ſhall in all things behave themselvs accordingly ..."

William Penn (1644-1718), first letter to the Lenni Lenape (or Delaware Indians), dated in the Quaker manner: 18th 8mo 81 (Old Style/Julian Calendar, 18th day, 8th month [October], 1681; equivalent to New Style/Gregorian Calendar, August 18, 1681). Transcription from a scanned (digitalized) copy of Penn's original hand-written text provided by the HSP (the Historical Society of Pennsylvania), keeping Penn's own orthography and spelling: freinds = friends, ſhall = shall, themselvs = themselves, etc.

Imagine this world busy with all beings

Imagine this world busy with all beings
(all of us) appreciating the best in one another,
encouraging the expression of our deepest, most
feeling and caring humanity.

The most valuable gift of our teachers

The most valuable gift of our teachers
is perhaps
not the answers they offer,
but the respectful attention they give
to the questions they articulate and address,
inspiring and challenging us
to grapple
earnestly
with those issues ourselves.

I knew them

I knew them
when we were all younger
(thirty years younger).
And they were troubled but still filled with hope
they sometimes could feel, although
at times, the world was too black for even that.
Young and passionate.
Then not so young and yet passionate.
Still later, no longer young but still quite passionate.

And now, I learn today they both are dead.
I read obituaries and old reports.

It is true that we all shall die
one day or another
but this seems irrelevant
somehow.

They have been in my thoughts for years
and are there now, with warmth and
a friendship that outlives their lives.

Being glad to have known them
rubbing elbows
in the struggle for air and free breathing.

Home

I climb the highest wave
hoping not to crash
but home at least
I melt in my lover's arms
filled with the cooing of my dove-heart and
the harmonies of a lullaby murmuring
murmuring complete security and
love-filled peace.

At the dawn

She opens her heart
and shows its inner recesses and petals
fragrant and vibrant;
I grow faint.

I was awakened during the night

I was awakened during the night
last night
to the gentle sensation
of a head of hair
against my fingers
and it occurred
to me
that the world
could be empty of all sensation
could be instead a world of rocks
insensate
that there might have been
no consciousness at all
but here was the awe-
filled reality of
awareness of
the sensation of hair.
I returned to sleep
joyously calm.

Joy

Joy
bubbling
gently
quietly,
screaming
in its fullness,
wet
sweet.
Let war
and hatred
melt
swallowed
in love
transformed
in tenderness.
Let fear
and anger
wash
to blinding light
in bliss.

We think of the world in a metaphor

We think of the world in a metaphor
which places the world
and each and all of us
as well
in some light or another.
Each metaphor
an extended caricature
highlighting some features,
ignoring others.
Who takes
a caricature for a
portrait? Who takes a
portrait for the
person portrayed?

Methodological yearning

Methodological yearning
is not dogmatic;
it looks beyond:
to make the process of yearning itself
different for us,
to have us experience yearning
differently,
to bring us to be in a new relationship
with the process of yearning,
to have us be beyond yearning
as it is usually experienced.

Mind grown small

Mind grown small
feeding on obtuse worries and plans
covers an unquenched longing
in heart and soul.
Forget worries and satisfy thirst.

Mind grown particularly petty,
feasting joyously on the misery of another.
Tasting the power
of foisting great torment on another
is exquisitely delicious to such a mind,
to such a heart,
sadly caustic in its inconsolable bitterness.
Time to crawl out of the petty box.

The great hall

The great hall of consciousness
            is empty;
no person to be found:
an empty hall
sweetly permeated with
the light clarity of wisdom,
            with
                        caring good-will,
compassion
bathed s p a c i o u s l y
in this smooth current
of radiant warmth.

Moon floating on the pond

Moon floating on the pond
dances with lilies in the night;
this heart sings of flowers
fragrant in full bloom.

When the short-sighted perspective

When the short-sighted perspective
presents itself
and we can let it arise
and dissipate and disappear
it does not drag anything along in its wake
still
the wave may be savored as it flows through,
may be presented as a visa is shown at borders.
Such a visa fits into our pocket
while we do not fit into it.

Crawling out of a small box

Crawling out of a small box
is the only way.
Otherwise we stay small,
our own thoughts remain
confined,
our breathing shallow, our air stale, our vision
myopic, distorted.
A new issue beyond
what we are trapped
into focusing on
can pry open this
box-container
and invite us to the inner palace
of our vibrant consciousness,
to a greater
vision and understanding.

Reaching out

Emotional rains creating mires of mind-mud fall,
making movement of body or mind tedious,
dark nights blacken the skies,
hibernation suddenly strikes us
as an alluring plan,
closing off our natural
inclination to live;
afraid of rejection, we withdraw first,
closing off our natural
yearning for human contact.
Here our longings lie hopeless
in deep-slime despondency.

Here our deepest soul
despite that, precisely because of that
reaches out for love
refuses to die
refuses to give up
refuses the pit.

Night ends
 night ends
not with a daybreak lightning bolt but
     with a tender a whimsical
          a whispering yearning.

Power of the now, prison of the now

The power of the now imprisons in the now,
but is presented glowingly, persuasively,
as the perfect path for the spiritually minded.
Be here now, as a proposal,
is certainly helpful for some sometimes,
as when lost in the past or future.

It doesn't help if lost, if locked, in the present ⁓
where all thoughts of past or future
are poison to be avoided ⁓
with no possibility of seeing
what we might like more
    than what is happening
        here and now,
    than how we are dealing with that,
        here and now.

Here, no possibility of remembering loving moments
and friendships that have changed through time,
of imagining what might bring us fulfillment in life.

Giving such power to the now does not permit us
to get an overview of our life and what is
most satisfying in it, or most frustrating in it,
or what we would find of great value
to continue, to change, to begin, or to end
at least, as *now* is usually contrasted with *then*, where
to be within this tiny *now* is to be locked in the present
with no greater appreciation of the process, the flow,
of our life than of its, a bee ⁓ a limited being
with little practical wisdom, prudence, or intelligence,
with little memory and no capacity for learning,
to use an ancient example from the *Metaphysics*
    of The Philosopher, Aristotle.

The power of process transcends the power of now.

VI. Restlessness Ceases

Restlessness ceases

Uparujjhati uddhaccaṃ
kukkuccaṃ parihīyati
cetanā cetanā yeva
ariyaṃ saccaṃ sukhaṃ mano.

Anattā khalu saṅkappā
suñño so paccayāsayo
ānāpāno va kāyamhi
annaṃ kho dhammapīti me.

Restlessness ceases
remorse is abandoned
thinking is just thinking;
truth is noble ∼ the heart's at ease.

Plans surely have no owner
quite empty is that realm of conditioning;
in the body there is breathing, in and out ∼
the drink of *dhamma* is indeed my nourishment.

*A poem composed in traditional Pāli meter, in the
style of ancient Udāna verses, expressions of intense
experience. The Pāli text is given here in romanized
transliteration, followed by an English rendering.*

121

To Ms. Kitty

Petted   the cat purrs contentedly.

Pushed away
by firm hand
by gruff voice   she turns away, then looks back
                        turns around and walks off
                                to the next reality
                                        easily
                        letting go of unwelcoming spaces.

All paths

All paths
that lead
        inwards and onwards
        in tenderness and in love
surely show their worth.

Here we may see the nurturing of
the most subtle awareness,
the knowing heart,
the aware state of mind,
in one vocabulary, bodhicitta.

Here is an awakening of our deepest being,
the birth of richly vibrant living,
the nourishing of our very soul,
the blossoming eruption of heart-wisdom,
the gradual cultivation of our precious heart-mind.

The flower

The flower
      wide-open to the warming sun
shuts up tight
      against the cold-night wind.

Karuṇa-pati, The Master of Compassion, asks:
Is one less beautiful than the other?

The Commentary says at this point:
The flower is our tender heart.

Your anger

Your anger
slashes through me, sabre-sharp.
I cry for the two of us.

Remembrance of warmth leads to
hopes of a rebirth and
a rekindling of those now-gone,
once harmonized feelings.
Here, hope is a fish-hook in our heart!

I see no limits

I see no limits to this pain I feel.
This love is one with the hurt
                          pain
                          torment here.
Sad is this growing separate
where once there was oneness.
I see you clearly
with love that breathes through all
       my body
I cannot remove you from
even one cell of my being.
Else, I am empty.
So many tears.

In the end, energies exhausted,
a reign of fatigue ⁓
a calm soft quiet.
Blessèd be fatigue.
Gentle slow breaths.

Active patience

The pain
the looking away
the slip into oblivion

the dark pit
the lost soul
the helplessness

the giving up
the letting go

the sense of clouds, of fog
the sense of time
the sense of limit

the sense of end
the sense of direction

the will to look

the joy of change

the strength to look
the sight of progress

the energy to flow
the harmony
the nonresistance
the welcoming

the unlocking
the floating
the freedom.

We want not to see

We want not to see what we take to be painful or ugly.
So we don't look.
From not looking comes not seeing.
From not seeing comes not knowing.
From not knowing comes lack of confidence.
From lack of confidence come brittleness, fragility,
  insecurity.
From brittleness and such comes fear.
From fear comes defensiveness.
From defensiveness comes hostility.
From hostility comes lack of understanding of others.
From lack of understanding comes lack of compassion.
From lack of compassion comes superficiality of
  relationship.
From superficiality of relationship comes frustration in the
  sphere of love.
From love frustration comes pain.

Not wanting to see pain or ugliness, we close ourselves in,
  creating some of the very pain we will later find
  ourselves experiencing or engaged in a further effort to
  avoid experiencing.

When we see that this is the price we pay for not looking,
  we are more willing to look even at what we take at first
  glance to be painful.

Do what teaches

Do what teaches.
Leave behind what reteaches what you already know.
Watch energy born of fear, worried energy, energy for
    keeping us in place, for locking out the unknown.
Dive into the void.

Learning to face what is difficult,
    we come to see what brings with it
    something strikingly unpleasant, painful.

We see what the whole situation calls for, rather than
    focusing on what we happen to want at the moment.

We travel through many varied
spaces, places, experiences, situations,
using whatever comes along to grow from,
to learn through, to appreciate.

Then it doesn't matter much what
in particular comes along.
We become a chameleon that lets itself be fully absorbed
into each experience, in sympathy with each new situation,
and yet the chameleon goes on.

There is this resonating, this sympathizing, in experience
more and more deeply.

Recollections

Recollections of
>the you you were and the you they saw you as,
>the beliefs you held,
>the feelings you felt.

Just recollections.
You don't know yourself anymore ～
live, learn.
>>Open-eyed, just seeing what is,
>>grounded in awareness,
>>grounded anywhere,
>>grounded everywhere.

Groundless traveler always at home.

Extended families

Beneficial extended families
allow a vision
opening otherwise trapped
constrained misunderstandings.

A small lad, a pre-toddler,
sits on the floor,
near relatives gathered there.

In walks his daddy, haggard
and irritable after a long
day at work. The boy feels
the tension vibrate through his body.

Mommy immediately becomes
agitated and disturbed. A double
dose of unpleasantness for the lad.

Then, as he glances up, he sees
his granddad looking at him,
with peace, and love, and calm
in his eyes, on his face, through his body.
The small boy realizes the tension
is not his, not him.

Record-player needle

When she first learned to read
when her father would take the family
out for errands, for a Sunday ride,
she would see words everywhere,
on store fronts, on signs,
on billboards.

It was so exciting to be able to
interpret what she saw with her eyes
and have words in her mind
and expressed through her voice.

Her father exclaimed,
"Who vaccinated *her* with a
record-player needle?"

Snuggle bunnies not so long ago

Vital are the love needs of snuggle bunnies.
Snuggle bunnies yearn
for touch, for gentle firm
secure touch
wanting human warmth
acceptance protection
appreciation safety.
With this then
effortlessly
cooing comes bubbling forth
radiant smiles
profound well-being
peacefulness
snuggle bunnies bathed in love
soul nourishment.

It's not so long ago,
I held you in my arms.
You slept head heavy against my shoulder,
your little feet not reaching down to my waist.
The night was dark and you,
after so many tears,
quiet,
calm.
It was not so long ago
and yet
I cannot bring back the
smell then of your flesh,
so reassuring,
my belovèd first-born.

I love you where there is no language

I love you where there is no language:
in the silence where we two see
all realities in their flow.
We look together and see what is going by
and accept all there is to accept,
which is, all there is, all.
If we touch by means of the body-sense
it is not *in order to*
BECOME close:
we are already as one:
we have already been through some of the
same spaces of consciousness.
We have looked at each other
and seen ∼ beyond
all manifestation, beyond
each moment of consciousness ∼ the other,
resting open and loving,
fully accepting, fully understanding,
fully feeling, sensing, and thinking.
We look at each reality as it is ∼ even
at thoughts of This is mine ∼ as not belonging to anyone.
You bring to me, for me to see, a light of life, and
there is joy in the seeing of this visible energy.
The light is ownerless,
it goes through "our" awareness:
you are illuminating, my shining being, my deva,
and you are
neither within or without.
In joy and love I lower my head towards you,
and I say Namas te.

To the belovèd

To the belovèd,
Ishq'allah,
Krishna,
Holy YOU

I live in YOU breathe me
                    in
                    and out
                    and in I live
                    through YOU nourish me
                            YOUR energy
gives me life I grow in joy
                    feeling YOU in me, YOU
                            before me, YOU
                            around me, YOU
YOU
        are limitless
            energy itself
            life in form
                in flow
                    changing
                    growing
                    evolving
                            the beauty of life.
THIS totality-in-movement
        full
        entire
        complete
                    answers all demands effortlessly
                        with what already manifests
                                    YOU.

I love you, I mean

I love you, I mean
I feel good
about me and about us.

The world is good, I mean
I feel secure.

Or, with more acute attention
to experiences at these times:

I feel love for you when I
am content and happy
with what I am experiencing,
with how I feel we are with one another.

And I feel that the world is good when I
feel secure in my situation,
free from a sense of imminent danger or destruction
of what I hold dear.

"Explanations exist; they have existed for all times, for there is always an easy solution to every human problem ⁓ neat, plausible, and wrong."
Henry L. Mencken (1880-1956), "The Divine Afflatus," *New York Evening Mail*, November 16, 1917; in H. L. Mencken, *Prejudices: Second Series* (1920), p. 158; phrasing varied through editions; quoted here from H. L. Mencken, *A Mencken Chrestomathy* (1949), p. 443.

The simple and the simplistic

We may well yearn for a sense of being one,
the urge to merge and dissolve, reflections of a yearning
that we be one, and that all the universe be one,
the urge for a world simple, peaceful, even blissful.
And yet when we stay singularly simple
we may ask if in that we are simply being
simplistic and confused, naïve and silly.

In contrast to this merging, in great articulate intimacy
we are two people appreciating one another,
truly seeing one another
in most-tender and rarely-shown-to-others ways.
There is a defenselessness and gentle vulnerability
we show one another at such times.
How we touch one another, interact,
resonate in this very palpable relatedness,
allows recognition of our individuality and closeness,
where all of our subtle and powerful differences
are seen, perceived, appreciated ⁓ a dance guided by
history, personality, values, with improvised movements
inspired by the fully alive experiencing of each moment.

Beyond couples are even greater complexities of life,
with many influences on any given particular scenario.
Replacing, then, the urge for a simple blissful fog,
perhaps we had best take a step back
look at our world from a wider perspective
before jumping to conclusions
that will drive us into even greater problems
into even more complex problems demanding
that we free ourselves from our urge to become simpletons
in the service of lazy blind simplicity.

Through the seasons

Passion love begins in flames.
Extinguished, it burns down to embers
then ashes.
Along the way, burning stinging
tears down the face.

Spring. Excitement, longing, hope.
Summer. Joy, love, bliss.
Autumn. Disappointment, loss, endings.
Winter. Hibernation, awaiting, rebirths.

VII. Understanding Within and Without

Understanding within and without

We can see how we think feel act
by noticing ourselves in focused detail ∽
a traditional meditative self-awareness practice.

We may be blind to certain features
of our own psychology ∽
and yet, as noted long ago (Matthew 7:3-5) ∽
we can see others' foibles and faults quite clearly!

Right then, lassies! Right then, lads!

And so to appreciate the ways of humans,
we may have the distance to recognize these
easier when they are shown to us by others, in others ∽
an inter-personal meditation practice.

We can use this ∽ not fight it or moralize against it ∽
to see first "out there" and, then,
to recognize the same "in here" ∽
these two domains of being mindful
both leading to appreciation of our shared humanity!

Let us not forget, though, it is quite easy to notice *there,*
yet manage to forget to look *here,*
only then to notice the same *here!*
and so easy
to keep our self-image pure since unexamined!

An early Indic source of this teaching is the Pāli Canon (the *Ti-pitaka* or *Three Baskets*). In its *Satipaṭṭhāna Sutta* (*Discourse on the Foundations of Mindfulness*), the tenth discourse of the *Majjhima-nikāya* (*Middle Length Collection*), within the *Sutta-piṭaka* (*Discourse Basket*), at vol. 1, pp. 55-63 (MN.i.55-63), is this same contrast of "inner" and "outer" mindfulness (at p. 56). A recent discussion of this distinction is in Chapter 11 ∽ "Inter-Personal Mindful-ness Practice (IPMP)" ∽ of M. Ginsberg, *Calm, Clear, and Loving*.

The heart pulls us on

The heart pulls us on to live.
How can we refuse it?
By being heartless.

Half-hearted, I rest alone. It is only a transient stage.
My fulfillment lies in the summer of rebirth,
when I sense you intimately fully.
'Til then I am envious most of all of you,
who are always close to you.

How does the heart open?

Sometimes it's so intense, with chest-shaking sobbing.
Breathless tightness and its explosive release.
A deep relaxing in the chest, through the body.
A glowing peace, a bathing in the heart's golden radiance.
All-open calm, the full body and mind
floating, buoyant in sweet ease.

Sometimes it is a very easy and non-strained
and gentle process:
like the melting of snow on a warm spring day.

The heart pulls us on to live.
How can we refuse it?
By being heartless.

If only I could, I would

If only I could
give you bliss
fulfill your every yearning
satisfy your every need
soothe your every ache
heal your every wound
hold you in total safety
in total security
in total peace
change every bitter tear
of sadness
into a honeyed tear of joy
of love, of beauty
give you fulfillment
give you a grounding in security
warmed by my heart
and by my caring presence
give you completeness, contentment,
give you a safe haven
give you shelter from every tempest
give you peace.
(Oh, for a fairy godmother's wand!)

If only I could
(and here, a deeper wish)
take you beyond
even these joys
to the wonder of the radiant
seeing feeling
caring accepting
complete
marriage of insight and lovingkindness,
in a heartbeat
I would.

We can be feeling

We can be feeling how people are
rather than merely understanding
what they (their words) are saying.

The mind's limit is the imagination,
the heart's, fear.

If I misunderstand you,
I end up confusing myself.

We know the mind,
   more precisely the small, narrow heartmind,
and its knowing ～ knowledge;
and the heart,
   more precisely the great, wise heartmind,
and its knowing ～ understanding.

In deep relationship comes
fullness of heart not fullness of self.

We can see our pain

We can see our pain,
can notice what we are doing,
be able to describe it in great detail,
picking out many specific features
(while ignoring many others, as usual),
and still not know how to stop
creating even more pain.

As a child washing his hands
can feel and look and see the soaked sleeves of his shirt
and make no link, can see no connection
between the washing of his hands
and the wetness of those sleeves
(not appreciating the way the water drips down),

as a child who does not notice where she
throws off her sweater when warm, does not remember
throwing off her sweater at all,
and later recognizes it
when a teacher holds it up
in class asking whose it is,
is not able to prevent
other articles of clothing from showing up,
being found by the teacher, repeatedly,
so embarrassing when classmates giggle or stare.

What is missing
is noticing and remembering
the steps that lead to the pain
(the pain here: the uncomfortable wet shirt
or the embarrassment
at being seen as forgetful by classmates).

Until that is achieved,
until the sequence that leads to the problem
is recognized, appreciated, understood,
correction is next to impossible.

Pornography: "you can recognize it by the insult it offers, invariably, to sex, and to the human spirit. Pornography is the attempt to insult sex ... As soon as there is sex excitement with a desire to spite the sexual feeling, to humiliate it and degrade it, the element of pornography enters."
D. H. Lawrence (1885-1930), "Pornography and Obscenity," *This Quarterly* (Paris & Monte Carlo, 1929), pp. 17-27, at pp. 24,27; quoted from D. H. Lawrence, *Pornography and Obscenity* (1929), pp. 13,16.

Pornography and sacred sex

Sex and pornography ⁓
how can they even be in the same world?

When sex begins as a natural human need
to feel intimate union with another, culminating
in our heart-felt acceptance of that thus-special person,
coupled with a sense of being so honored, ourselves,
more fully than we otherwise ever experience; and
when sex is the dream of vibrant blossoming youth,
creating anticipatory reveries of bliss, joy, fulfillment,
a deep yearning that reaches out for intense connection ⁓

how is this turned into dirty smut,
something disgusting, repugnant, to be avoided
if not destroyed passionately ⁓ oh what a distortion
of sexual love ⁓ and how transformed
by filthy muck-magic into the most vile of things on earth?

Sex can threaten leaders wanting compliance from others.
Those in the throws of orgasm, then peacefully content,
empty of bellicose urges, experience a human freedom
that does not answer to any power.
They at such times may well sense clearly what is of value,
what is time spent in fulfilling, satisfying ways, and
what is boring babble groundlessly demanding obedience.

Pornography's distortion of sacred sexual intimacy,
striving to destroy this source of deep human satisfaction,
shows profound hatred of the body and its divine powers.
Pornography is anti-sex, anti-love.

146

Samsāra for men and women

Siddhārtha, when newly a first-time father,
calling out that a fetter was born to him
        this utterance understood as a naming ritual
        then taken to be the son's name: Rāhula
was capable of leaving his hours-old son,
out of compassion for and for the benefit of
the entire universe, the point is made,
striving and years later becoming the Buddha,
while at the same time Siddhārtha's wife,
        known in various traditional
        texts by the names of Bimbā or Yaśodharā,
        a new mother from then on
        more often referred to as Rāhulamātā,
        meaning Mother of Rāhula
surely could not have abandoned
a new-born babe so casually.

Some suggest that perhaps her way was even
more noble and compassionate
than Siddhārtha's is portrayed as being.

A path to awakening through human relationship.

Here Siddhārtha and little Rāhula
were perhaps both babes in the wood.

Perhaps they were not ready to tread, then and there,
the path to awakening through human relationship,
to recognize, without further ado, without further to do,
as is said, that samsāra is simply nirvāna misunderstood,
and that nirvāna is just samsāra truly understood.

The dross of sad pasts not yet gone

Mourning grief remorse guilt nostalgia
all see the past with sad significance
inviting seeking, investigation
into our values, our heart.

The alchemy of using the dross
to derive the blessings,
appreciating and refining our life.

Perhaps ultimately seeing
        its perfect perfection
      (its Apollonian-beautiful stable perfection) *and*
        its perfect imperfection pushing us challenging us,
and through that further alchemy, ultimately embracing
        its reassuring wholeness *and*
        its question-raising cracks
      (its Wabisabi-beautiful limping living imperfection).

Beauty in imperfection: the Japanese aesthetics of wabisabi
(侘寂).

Through the many years, if most fortunate

Through the many years, if most fortunate,
we have the opportunity of apologizing
for wrongs done
or being apologized to,
and of seeing the apologies
accepted.

Yet years may have gone by, suffering
impacting much of our lives,
tears, fears, regrets, remorse, rage, resentment.

So what is done is done, later apologies or no.

Still, what pain was felt through those years
may become faded in memory,
may be softened, sweetened
perhaps, even if not erased
by later apology.

Soft are your ways

Soft are your ways
and loving.
Few are your words but full of truth,
spoken from the heart.
Gentle and shy
I feel you reach out,
gingerly,
with love.
You are precious to me,
my friend.

Indra's net

Interconnected reality
forming a whole.
To see
first, a breath, its depth,
its coolness, its warmth.
Each moment, pleasant or not.
States of mind flavoring consciousness.
Thoughts, focal points in the flow.
Our past, coloring this entire pattern.
(Our parents, grandparents, and others,
all leaving their marks on our soul,
gentle or harsh, clear or confused.)
Our hopes and fears
for our future,
already woven into our present.
Meeting others,
their past, present, future,
all intermingling with ours.
Generations of personal history
and world events
in play,
in one interconnected reality.
Indra's net.

Full circle

When we come full circle
having reflected, analyzed, contemplated
the nature of consciousness,
having looked into our
innermost chambers,
and seen the workings and pathways
of our mind,
when we have taken this trip
and have returned home,
come back
full circle
we may sense, tasting the newness of the moment,
that it is not as it was.
We are not as we were.

Same context,
new awareness, mind, thoughts, responses,
moving to new clarity,
the circle opening into a helix,
into a liberating transformation.
Has it been, rather, a pointless voyage
that we soon forget?
Or, do we truly find ourselves different, transformed?
What in fact have we seen, discovered, appreciated?
Perhaps we have seen what centers us,
have seen what replaces needy hungry loneliness
with vibrant, satisfied fullness, rich solitude,
have seen what brings us agitation
    and what brings us calm,
have seen what brings us confusion
    and what brings us clarity,
have seen what brings us fright or anger or envy
    and what allows us to feel
sympathy, compassion, good-will, lovingkindness.
Perhaps we have seen
what we value and appreciate,
what makes us
feel at peace and fully alive.

We know the path

We know the path that is not a straight path;
we know that approaching the heart
that opening the heart
goes slowly, then quickly, or not at all,
goes in its own tempos, in its own directions.

We know the yearning that will not die
no matter what the pain,
no matter what the tearful sobbing.

We know the tenderness that is cautious;
we know the urge to hide, to stop,
the urge to close off, to close down.

We know the gentleness, the sense of caring,
the sense of touching another's soul
the sense of reaching out,
softly, gingerly, hesitatingly.

We know the path that is a long one
the path back to our source,
to our heart,
to our drive for life.

We know the wordless awe of human contact
so rare, so fragile, so promising,
so fleeting, so nourishing.
We know at times very little of how we shall go
but onwards we go, refusing to settle
for less than we need, for less than we deserve.

This is our human
strength and power.

Needs

Human needs may be denied or camouflaged
but they will retain nonetheless their full force.

On a physical level,
humans have a need for oxygen,
for space to move about in,
nutrition to eat, water to drink, for example,
to go to some quite basic considerations
on the physical level of our existence.

While in other ways, we have a need
for security,
a sense of well-being,
a place in our group,
respect and acknowledgment,
satisfaction and a sense of fulfillment,
loving care and tender touch,
a sense of how we contribute to those in our world,
whether intimates or acquaintances.

When we do not keep in the front of our minds
our needs
and those of people we are dealing with in life,
we may feel the impact of those needs
in ways that are hurtful,
harmful,
or simply confusing.

When someone threatens or criticizes
or attacks us
in word or deed
because feeling insulted
or not respected,
or in danger,
we may all act in the dark,
not appreciating the drive
to take care of personal needs
above all else,
even if not speaking or

thinking
of them
explicitly.

How are we to identify our needs?

We may be too precise: I need my father to love me
versus I need to feel loveable,
or, I need to receive high evaluations
in these studies or in my work
versus I need to feel competent and
to be seen as competent;
he needs to hear her apologize for insulting him,
or needs to feel respect reestablished
between him and her ⁓ both these though still stuck
to the particulars of that interaction ⁓ versus
he needs to feel respected.

Going to basic needs,
freed from a particular story
of how those needs might be satisfied,
we give ourselves
and others
a much greater flexibility
and adaptability about how to live life
respecting and satisfying all of our basic needs,
as they shift and change in importance or relevance
through life's contexts and unexpected turns.

Human needs may be denied or camouflaged
but they will retain nonetheless their full force.

Emergencies ～ the emerging of urgent needs

Chaos reigns, or so it seems.
People are anxious, worried, agitated, upset.
Some are angry and demanding.
Others, sad, crying, sobbing, moaning.
Some stand by stoically.
Most want things to be settled,
resolved,
determined,
want to close the chapter.
All forms of impatience, these.

Chaos, called an emergency,
is a fluid, creative moment,
where one organization of our lives
or relationship or family
is naturally dissolving,
unable to deal adequately with the current realities,
inviting more elegant, nuanced,
competent ways of continuing on, inviting more
skillful and beneficial patterns of process.

Here is the promise
that will not always come to fruition
automatically, easily, thoughtlessly.

Here is a time of powerful flux, of promising fluidity.
Here, the emerging of urgent needs
demands not only efficiency but also respectful
satisfaction of all that is important before us,
until now disregarded or intentionally denied,
and calls upon us to bring to bear
our kind awareness, our caring wisdom,
guiding this urgent emerging of new demands
for relating more harmoniously with one another
with fulfillment and respect for all.

Kindly aware

Kind awareness
occurs when we are aware

conscious, attentive, perceiving,
having familiarity with,
recognition of, and
sensitivity about,
having feeling, and understanding,
all together ∼
called jué in the speech of Chinese hermits ∼

in a way that is

wise, honest, reliable, good-willed, clear,
able to make whole, to make good, to perfect,
actively benevolent, skillful, apt, expert,
grounded, caring, and thorough,
all together ∼
called shàn in that same speech.

Kindly aware: juéshàn 覺善; in simplified characters, 觉善.

Natural compassion

Our natural open attentiveness,
kind, calm, and aware,
has us notice those
who lack relaxing refreshing calm,
who are pained,
distracted, worried, frustrated,
defensive, vengeful,
enraged, confused,
anguished, tormented.

Our minds
available to notice what there is to notice ∼
if not blocked,
pushing away awareness in a dualistic
"us-them" mind-set,
disregarding it because not "ours" ∼
we will easily notice this torment;

with our basic desire
that there be no torment,
here as well as elsewhere,
we sense the desire that this torment, too,
be terminated.

If not distorted, perverted into pity,
here is the natural
arising in kind awareness
of sympathy, of compassion.

Simple boredoms

Same old routines, same old patterns,
boring us to death.

And yet,
there is a knowing, a familiarity,
a not needing to work hard
to know the steps we are supposed to take next.

We can do it all by rote, without a thought,
living on automatic pilot, comfortable perhaps,
but zombie-like, half-dead, fully deadened.

Familiar but rigid is such a life
we have created for ourselves,
without verve, without vitality, a bit unreal.

This cage we find ourselves in
like all cages has a door and a lock
and a key to open up our reality
inviting us to spaciousness and interest and life.

From simple boredom to complex vibrancy
is not a long trip ～
it takes place with just one key step,
individual, specialized,
fitting into the locked situation,

one that is continuously new, fresh,
always but always add
an additional dimension
to our path, to our pattern, making it
more complex more intricate more involved
less like goose stepping and more like spinning free.

Unlocking the prison of routine, opening out, freeing
to the grand magnificence of freshly lived life ～
all this, our natural heritage as conscious living beings.

Thin is the line; nearby lies a new dimension

Appreciating life is
knowing how thin the line is
between joy and torment
between pleasure and displeasure.

The shift, the crossing of the line,
can happen quickly and unexpectedly.

In this same way, love and hate
are very close to one another,
fear and rage, too.

Our mundane emotions,
bouncing us
from sun-drenched mountain top
to somber shaded valley,
give us excitement, a sense of being alive
that we cannot deny, give us little rest,
inviting us to dance or to groan.

Far from all such pairs is a third option, a new dimension,
a quiet and a peace that we may have experienced in some
strange, unexpected context,
where we may not have identified it immediately,
but only later.

If we let ourselves breathe quietly
and just notice the soft life
within our body, freed momentarily from tasks
waiting to be addressed,
we may transport ourselves
in an instant to that spaciousness.

How to visit that consciousness
more regularly is a search
that many have devoted their lives to.

It is a search for a still-point allowing us
to appreciate the specifics and the patterns of our life.

Physical love

Touching.
Holding.
Cuddling.
Breathing
as one.
Flowing motion,
full harmonies.
Bodies
in
musicless
dance,
neither leading,
both alive with
movement.
Rhythms
of the
Universe.
Mystical
Union.

"I am certain of nothing but of the holiness of the Heart's affec-
tions and ... of all our Passions of Love ..."
John Keats (1795-1821), in a letter to Benjamin Bailey dated Novem-
ber 22, 1817.

Love

Love   is caring, good-will, warmth, gentleness.
Love   is active, not passive; it
       is what we do, not what happens to us.
Love   is coming to know the other, and it
       is respecting the other's yearnings,
       needs,
       personality.
Love   is attentive, appreciative, and caring.
Love   looks outward to the other and sees
       another individual,
       not a mirror image of ourselves.
Love   looks inward and sees
       the delicate intimacy of our connection,
       a combination of separateness and closeness.
Love   calls us
       to reach out,
       to seek understanding, to be understood,
       to find harmony and respect.
Love   is patient, enduring, persevering.
Love   is deeply engaged with heart-felt commitment
       when disharmonies reign,
       and flows gently and effortlessly
       when relationships are relaxed and easy
                   letting closeness blossom.
Love   is soulful intensity, and, as well, it is
       p a s s i o n a t e
       a p p r e c i a t i o n.

Index of Poems by Title and First Line

Cited by title
and by beginning phrase of first line, if distinct,
arranged alphabetically

Index of Names

Index of Names

About the author

Born in troubled times
(who isn't?)

in a caring hospital
(are all?)

still in a time of peace
(not the fortune of all)

soon transformed into war
(who lives a full long life
without living through one or more?),

in a time less tormented than others
(but more than still others,
no doubt),

living here and there
(some stay in place for a lifetime),

hearing stories of other harrowing times
(who who listens, doesn't?),

drawn to torment
(as many, for many different reasons)

and to joy
(many its forms).

This could also be stated
with some specifics made explicit,

as follows
(on the next page).

❧ About the Author ❧

MITCHELL GINSBERG was born at the then-still-existent & warmly-welcoming Women's Homeopathic Hospital, in Philadelphia (a.k.a. The City of Brotherly Love) ~ the day the very first SS-RSHA death-train transport of Jews from France (from Drancy, next to Paris, & from Compiègne) arrived at Oświęcim (Auschwitz; known then only in Drancy Yiddish slang as Pitchipoï, an empty name for an unknown destination) ~ some 16 weeks after December 7, 1941: the date of the bombing of Pearl Harbor, of Reich Chancellor Hitler's Night & Fog Decree (Nacht und Nebel Erlaß), & of the opening of Chełmno (Kulmhof), the first center for the systematic gassing to death of Jewish prisoners (in gas vans), soon eclipsed by the rather more efficient extermination camps of Auschwitz, Belzec, Sobibor, and Treblinka: all in all, a date that continues to live in infamy, in more ways than Franklin Delano Roosevelt had in mind.

After his birth into that loving & troubled world, Mitchell grew up in & near Philadelphia, learning East Coast irony & sharpness of tongue, if not wit. He did undergraduate studies in Romance Languages, Physical & Biological Sciences, & Philosophy, at the University of Pennsylvania (in West Philadelphia).

Following this were doctoral studies in Philosophy, Psychology, & French at the University of Michigan (in Ann Arbor), where he became acquainted with extremes of windy cold & humid heat, with intervening respites of the briefest of Springs & Autumns, all averaging out (mathematically, at least) to a surprisingly lovely Middle Path of temperature & weather (on paper).

While living in New England (New Haven & Cambridge) for most of the next decade, he taught as a university professor (Yale), did post-doctoral studies (MIT & Yale), & received extensive clinical experience & training in psychotherapy (Yale).

After advanced intense meditation practice & Buddhist studies in North America & Europe & being invited to become a teacher in 1975 in the Thai-Burmese Buddhist Meditation Tradition, he divided his time for the next years into the early 1980s primarily between France (Grenoble & Paris), Britain (Cornwall & Cambridgeshire), & California (Berkeley).

Through the decades, he has also held teaching, training, & academic & research positions in a number of academic departments at various American universities, affording him the pleasure of meeting some remarkable students & the subsequent joys of seeing some of these inspired individuals going on to make their own contributions to the worlds they have touched, with their own satisfactions in life.

Since 1982 he & his wife have lived in San Diego, where their two children were born & raised & became adults. During this time, in addition to academic positions, he has had a private practice as a licensed psychotherapist in California, done therapy supervision for therapists-in-training, & worked with organizations offering therapy & related psychological services to people having experienced abuse & torture in numerous countries around the globe.

More recently, he founded Wisdom Moon Publishing, LLC, & has worked as its Editor-in-Chief.

His published writings through the decades primarily investigate consciousness & the nature of experience, the mind, thinking, & the emotions, as well as issues focusing on language, logic, & translation theory, communication, & human interaction, including their roles in the world of psychotherapy.

Pax fluctuat nec mergitur.

Finis

www.ingramcontent.com/pod-product-compliance
Lightning Source LLC
Chambersburg PA
CBHW031509270326
41930CB00006B/318